2/75

Also by Zhores A. Medvedev

THE MEDVEDEV PAPERS (1971)
THE RISE AND FALL OF T. D. LYSENKO (1969)

A QUESTION OF MADNESS

A

QUESTION

OF

MADNESS

ZHORES A. MEDVEDEV

ROY A. MEDVEDEV

Translated from the Russian
by Ellen de Kadt

New York   *1971*

ALFRED·A·KNOPF

THIS IS A BORZOI BOOK
PUBLISHED BY ALFRED A. KNOPF, INC.

ISBN: 0-394-47900-9
Library of Congress Catalog Card Number: 75-179062

Manufactured in the United States of America
Published December 1, 1971
Second Printing, December 1971

Contents

A NOTE ON CHARACTERS

MANY people appear in the course of this narrative. The most prominent intellectuals are introduced on their first appearance. However, it may assist the reader to have a list of the 'doctors' and officials who played a part.

ANTONENKO, NINA PETROVNA—Chairman of the Obninsk City Soviet.

BONDAREVA, GALINA PETROVNA—Psychiatrist in charge of the wing where Zhores Medvedev was placed at the Kaluga Psychiatric Hospital.

KIRYUSHIN, Y. V.—Director of the Obninsk Psychiatric Clinic.

LEZNENKO, VLADIMIR NIKOLAEVICH—Director of the Kaluga Psychiatric Clinic.

LIFSHITS, ALEXANDER YEFIMOVICH—Head Doctor of the Kaluga Psychiatric Hospital.

PETROVSKY, B.—Minister of Health of the USSR.

SEREBRYAKOVA, ZOYA NIKOLAEVNA—Chief Psychiatric Specialist at the Ministry of Health of the USSR.

SHOSTAKOVICH, BORIS VLADIMIROVICH—Forensic psychiatrist of the Serbsky Institute.

SNEZHNEVSKY, A. V.—Chief Psychiatrist of the USSR Ministry of Health, Academician, Secretary of the Academy of Medical Sciences.

Zhores Medvedev

AUTHOR'S NOTE

THE author wishes to express his most profound gratitude to all those friends, acquaintances and strangers, at home and abroad, who by protesting in various ways against the inhumane use of medicine for political purposes, created a climate of opinion which meant freedom for him and hope for others illegally confined in psychiatric hospitals.

Roy Medvedev

INTRODUCTION

IN August–September 1970, my brother Zhores A. Medvedev wrote an account of certain events which are undoubtedly of public interest. I was also involved and kept a record of the whole episode for the benefit of our friends. My own notes include many details which are not described by my brother and so complete the picture of what took place. I have arranged the material as follows: Zhores describes events as he directly experienced and interpreted them; at certain points I interrupt his story with my own recollections. In order to avoid repetition, I have made several small cuts in my brother's part of the narrative.

R. A. M.

2 October 1970

A QUESTION OF MADNESS

1

Preparation of the 'Scenario'
April–May 1970

ZHORES MEDVEDEV

I was asked to forget what I am now about to describe. I agreed, but only under certain conditions. Now, three months after the main events of the story, it has become clear that the other side has not kept its part of the bargain, and this unties my hands. In these circumstances there can be no dilemma: one cannot conceal facts that are of such public importance.

As background to the events described here, I must begin with an unfortunate incident which took place two months earlier. At the end of February one of my friends felt in honour bound to tell me about a KGB search which had taken place at the flat of a scientist acquaintance (a mathematical physicist). My friend was particularly worried because he had lent his colleague a copy of my book *Fruitful Meetings Between Scientists of the World*,[1] and it had been confiscated along with several *samizdat* manuscripts.

I didn't know the man in question and hadn't given

---

[1] Published in the West, together with Medvedev's work on the problems of corresponding with people abroad (*Secrecy of Correspondence is Guaranteed by Law*), in one volume entitled *The Medvedev Papers* (Macmillan, 1971).

All footnotes, unless otherwise indicated, are the translator's.

permission for him to see the manuscript, but I was not alarmed by the fact that the KGB now had it. The confiscated work was not strictly speaking *samizdat* since it bore corrections in my own hand and was signed by me. Also this draft had been completed in the spring of 1968 and wasn't in any way secret. The subject of the book, the very real problem of co-ordinating scientific research on a world-wide scale, is a topic of discussion among scientists in many countries. The 1968 version was only a preliminary draft, a basis for discussion and not yet intended for publication; over the next two years I had frequently discussed it with colleagues and made many revisions. At the end of 1968 I had been asked to adapt one of the chapters for publication in a Moscow journal but I considered this to be premature. Many people read the manuscript in the course of those two years, but because of the precautions I had taken it had not become the property of *samizdat* (that is, it was not being copied out and circulated by third parties). All the people who read it had been given signed copies only, and there were not many of these—certainly the number of copies available was well within the limits of what it would be normal to circulate for preliminary professional discussion. Perhaps it hadn't been picked up by *samizdat* because the number of these copies was too small to precipitate the *samizdat* chain reaction, or possibly because the subject was too specialised.

I meant to get down to serious revision of the manuscript in 1971 and in the meantime quietly to gather additional data as well as other people's views and comments. The book was not intended only for scientists or for some special liberal strata of the intelligentsia. I was also interested in the reaction of Party and government people, and it might have been useful to discuss several sections even with officials of the KGB. When it was ready, I hoped to submit the book through the normal channels to Glavlit[1] and get its authoritative verdict about the contents. I might now, however, be summoned and asked to explain how the unfinished manuscript came to be found among some *samizdat* items confiscated by the KGB.

But March passed without incident, which made it possible to assume that although they never returned the manuscript it at least had not aroused any special interest in those expert quarters. By April I was preoccupied with other problems and had almost forgotten about the incident.

On 8 or 9 April I received an unexpected phone call from the Obninsk City Soviet[2] and was told that its chairman, Nina Petrovna Antonenko, urgently wanted to see me. I was naturally curious about the reason for this summons, but the secretary would only say that it was about something very important. I went there immediately and was received on arrival by Mrs Antonenko. During my seven years in Obninsk, I had never been inside her office before.

It turned out that she wanted to discuss the behaviour of my elder son. He was a student in the tenth class, and in the last two or three years the boy had indeed been a cause of concern both to his teachers and to his parents. Having reached the so-called 'awkward

---

[1] Glavlit is the name of the chief organ of censorship in the USSR. For the origin of the name, see *The Medvedev Papers*, 11 note.

[2] The council of the town in which Zhores Medvedev lives. A City Soviet is the main government and administrative body in local government.

age', he had begun to do badly in the eighth class and his conduct both at school and at home decidedly changed for the worse. His general behaviour was what abroad would be called 'hippie'. His reaction to attempts at persuasion and discipline by the school and his parents was to run away to the South in the summer of 1968, where for two weeks he lived at the seaside, keeping himself by selling part of his stamp collection. In the Crimea, the police are on the lookout for these numerous teenage 'fugitives' and return them to their parents; this is precisely what happened to our son. But when this escapade was repeated with the same result, we felt compelled to turn to a psychiatrist for advice; that is, we took the natural step for parents baffled by unaccountable changes in the character of their teenage child.

The psychiatric examination did not reveal any basic change affecting his psyche or his mind, and judging by the explanations of the doctor, all it amounted to was a premature hormonal development. As a result he couldn't at present adequately restrain or control his emotions but as he grew up, given the proper supervision, this uninhibited behaviour would pass.

Antonenko made her own observations and gave me some pedagogical advice. As a warning she then told me about the unhappy fate of the son of the Secretary in charge of ideological questions at the Obninsk Party Committee. This boy, together with other youths, had recently been convicted of a criminal offence. After this she informed me that on the following day I was to go and see Comrade Vovk at the Kaluga[1] Department of Education to discuss my son's behaviour.

[1] The regional capital.

'See for yourself,' she said, showing me a letter on official stationery.

The letter from the regional Department of Education was addressed to the chairman of the Obninsk City Soviet and asked her to ensure that Z. A. Medvedev would come to Kaluga at 11.30 on the following day to discuss the problem of his son, Alexander. But I wasn't free on that day because I had an appointment in Moscow at the Academy of Medical Sciences (AMS) with regard to my complaint, sent in many months before, about being illegally dismissed from my post as head of a laboratory. I told Antonenko this and asked her to arrange the trip to Kaluga for another day. She at once rang the Kaluga Department of Education, but they insisted that I must go to see them the next day. I then agreed to the appointment itself but said that my wife would go in my place. This solution for some reason very much displeased Mrs Antonenko. She began to try to convince me that it would not be the same thing at all, that they particularly wanted to talk to the father. I explained that my wife knew about all the problems of our son, also that she was a professional woman and had been a member of the children's commission of her trade union committee, but Antonenko still insisted that I must go. This kind of discrimination between mother and father was incomprehensible. I asked whether any other parents had been summoned to Kaluga for this meeting, but it turned out that I was the only one. This was bewildering because my son was hardly the worst student even in his particular class, let alone in the school or the city as a whole. Antonenko explained that right now they were particularly interested in the children of prominent parents. I could only shrug, because at the time my 'prominence' was not very enviable; I was simply out of a job.

The conversation ended in compromise. If I could get the Academy of Medical Sciences to put off my visit to them for a day, then I would try and go to Kaluga. From the City Soviet I went straight to the director of my son's school to find out the reasons for the summons to the Department of Education. But it turned out that nobody from Kaluga had made inquiries about my son at his school. And so the whole thing began to look very odd. Why had it been arranged through the Chairman of the City Soviet and not directly through the school? Why were they so adamant about seeing the father and not the mother? And why not send for our son as well, who was after all already seventeen. But since I didn't want to make someone in Kaluga sit and wait to no purpose, I sent a telegram to Vovk saying that because of my appointment in Moscow, I was unable to come.

Approximately ten days later Vovk rang me herself and asked me to come to Kaluga the next day. The conversation ran roughly as follows:

Medvedev: I don't see any serious reason to go to Kaluga to talk about my son. I haven't been approached either by the director of his school or by the Obninsk Department of Education. Besides, in a month the school year will be over, and he will no longer be within your jurisdiction. My son has only one problem right now—to finish school, and his teachers think that although he won't do brilliantly, he will manage to get his certificate. I fail to understand your concern.

Vovk: We have important reasons for wanting to see you. It's in your own interest. Surely you are not indifferent to the fate of your son?

Medvedev: But what do you want to see me about? Can't you explain briefly on the phone? It takes a long time to get to Kaluga, you know—and you may not want to see me for more than ten minutes.

Vovk: It will take more than ten minutes—and we have only limited funds for long-distance telephone calls.

Medvedev: Give me your telephone number, put down your receiver, and I'll ring you back. Then we can talk for as long as necessary at my expense. You ought in any case to tell me what it's all about so that I can think it all over in advance.

Vovk: We're worried about several aspects of your son's behaviour. We have received certain information and don't exclude the possibility of sending him to a psychiatrist. We have invited a leading Kaluga psychiatrist, Comrade Leznenko, to the Department. He is extremely experienced and he will talk to you at length about your son and make a lot of valuable suggestions. We now take this kind of approach with difficult youngsters and we are getting good results.

I told him that we had previously consulted a psychiatrist about our son. Right now, just before his final examinations, to take him to a psychiatrist or to go to Kaluga for psychiatric advice didn't make much sense.

The reasons behind such strange and insistent invitations to Kaluga were becoming obvious. The intention was to set up a psychiatric examination not for the son but for the father—which is why they were not

interested in seeing my wife. It was by now a notorious
practice that persons who aroused the displeasure of the
authorities without actually breaking the law could
suddenly be made to undergo psychiatric examinations. It was usually done on the pretext of a routine
check of fitness for military service and the victims
were summoned to their local draft office for this purpose. This had recently happened to a friend of mine in
Moscow. For a long time he had been feuding with
the post office about the disappearance of registered
letters he had sent abroad. After he had tried to serve a
writ on them through the courts he was summoned
by his draft board for a medical examination which
turned out to be in fact psychiatric. There was also
a certain case in which a person known for his dissident
views was taken from the draft board straight to a
mental hospital. General Petr Grigorenko and Ivan
Yakhimovich, whose writings had been published
abroad, are being held in mental hospitals.[1] I also
knew of attempts to dismiss works by victims of
Stalin's terror about the forced labour camps as
'psychopathological'. At several meetings to discuss
ideological questions, it had been stated that a number
of authors, because of the suffering they had experienced, had developed 'obsessions' with such
themes.

It looked, therefore, as if this kind of psychiatric
'scenario' was in store for me as well. But since a summons to the draft office was ruled out in my case,
someone had conceived the bright idea of inviting me
to the Department of Education, since nothing could

---

[1] Yakhimovich was released in the spring of 1971.

be more expedient than to play on a father's natural feelings for his son.

My suspicions soon grew more positive. About two weeks later Antonenko again asked me to come to the City Soviet, this time to talk about my employment situation. Since I had been without work for more than a year, the authorities had a legal right to demand an explanation.

When I arrived at the appointed time the next day, Antonenko was not alone in her office. Next to her at her desk sat a stranger, whom she introduced as an official from the regional Department of Education. I was never, however, told his name. He was supposedly going to ask me questions about my son.

The conversation about employment did not take long. Antonenko read out extracts from some new decree providing for stiffer penalties against persons evading work. After this she demanded that I explain such a long period 'outside the collective'. I tried to show that I could hardly be regarded as a person who 'evaded work', since I had been illegally dismissed from my institute (in violation of the regulations about posts to which appointments are made by open competition). I had appealed to the Academy of Medical Sciences and to the Obninsk Procurator[1] many times with requests for reinstatement, but all to no purpose. For almost a year the Institute had refused to give me the essential documents I needed in order to apply for a post in any other scientific institution. I was at last given these documents but only after three

[1] The Procurator's office in the Soviet Union is concerned not only with prosecution but also has supervisory functions—investigating citizens' complaints, etc.

directives to that effect from the Procurator and the AMS, and even then they were full of inaccuracies. Recently I had applied for a position as a Senior Research Fellow in biochemical genetics at the Institute of Medical Genetics in Moscow, and was waiting to hear about this. I could scarcely be described as a person who was evading work. And if the City Soviet could help—for example, by getting me reinstated in my post in the only institute in Obninsk in my field— I would be very grateful.

The conversation then turned to my son. At first the nameless official from the Department of Education restricted himself to educational matters, but towards the end of our conversation he involuntarily gave away his true function.

'You have another younger son?' he asked. 'And how is he getting on at school? Are there any complaints about his behaviour?'

I replied that my younger son was an excellent student and his behaviour both at home and at school was completely satisfactory.

'I also gather that you have a twin brother. Does he have any children?'

'My brother has one son. He's just finishing the fifth class.'

'Excuse my curiosity,' he went on, 'but how is your brother's son doing at school? Twins often have similar problems with their children, you know.'

These questions made it completely obvious that the stranger was no educationalist but a psychiatrist who was cautiously trying to explore my family background.

Soon after this episode I heard one more disturbing

piece of news. Someone had gone to the Institute of Medical Radiology, where I had been employed until March 1969, and asked several former colleagues 'confidentially' about what the atmosphere had been like in my laboratory there. He was particularly interested to know whether or not there had been any conflicts between me and my former colleagues.

At the beginning of May I was asked to come for a talk about my son by the director of the Obninsk Psychiatric Clinic, Y. V. Kiryushin. This time, however, I was not particularly worried by the summons because it was Kiryushin whom I had previously consulted about the changes in my son's behaviour. He had given specific advice at the time and had every reason to check on the boy's development. What is more I had known Kiryushin before he became a local psychiatrist. His wife, who worked in our department at the Institute, was a sister of a good friend of mine in Moscow. I had even thought of consulting Kiryushin confidentially about several legal questions relating to psychiatry.

The Obninsk Psychiatric Clinic consisted of an outpatient department and a small hospital with twenty-five to thirty beds, on the whole for not particularly serious cases. My son and I went to Kiryushin's waiting-room in the outpatient department, but the nurse on duty said that he was expecting us in his office in the hospital. The three of us talked there together for a few minutes, and then Kiryushin said that he wanted to speak to my son alone. I left his office and sat on a chair in the corridor. After about two minutes a nurse came up to me, said it was not permitted to wait there and that Kiryushin wanted me to go to the waiting-room. She opened a door with a special key, led me through a bathroom, opened the next door and left me there—in a small room. I sat down and started to gaze out of the window, waiting for Kiryushin to finish his talk with my son. After about fifteen minutes I saw my son leave the building and head for home, but no one had come for me. I decided to go back to Kiryushin, but the door of the room turned out to be locked. It had been snapped shut by a standard lock of the sort which could only be opened with a special key, like the rectangular ones used on railway trains. After twenty more minutes had gone by, I began to feel very anxious. The double-framed window was covered by a solid grille and was locked. I had clearly walked into a trap. There was no response to my banging on the door, and in any case, the room was cut off from the corridor by the bathroom. Obviously it was not a waiting-room for visitors but a changing-room for patients. After admission, this is where they were undressed, led into the bath and afterwards given hospital garments. I had come here of my own free will—and everyone knows why people come to psychiatric hospitals. I began to bang on the door as hard as I could but very soon stopped, realising that it might be used against me if my confinement in this little room was not simply a mistake on the nurse's part. Kiryushin of course was an acquaintance but hardly a friend, and he might well have been party to the plot. He was a Party member, and his political loyalty was beyond doubt. Perhaps right now he was ringing the appropriate department, informing them that Medvedev was in the hospital and could be found in the patients' dressing-room.

I had to think of some other way out. I began to look carefully at the lock. It was a Yale-type lock which snapped to automatically when the door was closed, but there was a keyhole on both sides of the door. I tried to turn the lock by squeezing in two ordinary keys from the bunch in my pocket, but it didn't yield. It was becoming very warm; the clinic was still heated because the beginning of May had been cold. I threw my coat on the chair and suddenly remembered that there was a large pocket-knife in the inside pocket which I used for pruning in my garden. With it I began to force back the tongue of the lock in the small gap between the door and the door jamb. The lock began to give, and after several attempts the door opened. I got out through the door to the corridor in the same way. From the corridor I walked into the visitors' waiting-room, where a nurse, seeing a stranger dressed in an overcoat, showed me out into the street.

But this was not the end of the psychiatrists' concern about the health of my son. On the morning of 30 May Kiryushin rang me again. He earnestly tried to persuade me that my son must be seen by an experienced psychiatrist who was coming to Kaluga for consultations with local doctors. Kiryushin had already made arrangements with the head doctor of the Kaluga hospital—and if I came with my son at twelve o'clock the next day, the Moscow professor would give him a thorough examination.

I wanted to know the name of the Moscow professor, but Kiryushin couldn't remember it. I then expressed doubts about the advisability of a consultation with a doctor whose name I didn't know, especially since on 21 May my son had certain commitments at his school in connection with preparations for the school-leaving ceremonies.

Kiryushin rang again in the afternoon. He now remembered the name of the doctor—it was a Professor Melekhov, one of the greatest psychiatric specialists in the USSR. I thanked him for his trouble and asked him to put it all in writing. My wife went to fetch this document. However on the official form, with Kiryushin's stamp and signature, there was no mention of Melekhov. The text was as follows:

> To the Head Doctor of the Kaluga Psychiatric Hospital, Comrade Lifshits,
> In accordance with arrangements made with the head of the Kaluga clinic, I hereby send Alexander Zhoresovich Medvedev for consultation.

By now I was already an old hand at this game. I immediately rang a friend in Moscow connected with psychiatry, and found out that Dmitri Yevgenevich Melekhov really did exist and that he was a prominent and respected psychiatrist. He was now seventy years old and retired, though he sometimes gave consultations in Moscow hospitals. Within an hour I also found out that Melekhov never gave consultations in Kaluga, did not intend going there on 21 May and had not been invited to do so.

2

The Beginning of the Operation—29 May

ON Friday, 29 May, my younger son finished school and began his holidays. In the tenth class they had stopped work a week earlier, and my elder son was planning a fishing trip over the weekend. We had just sat down to dinner in a mood of celebration when the telephone rang. It was Kiryushin again. Sounding rather anxious, he asked me to come and see him at the clinic immediately.

'It is very important and has to do with your son.'

'Has something happened?' I asked. 'Sasha feels very well and is just about to go off fishing.'

'It is so important that I cannot discuss it with you on the telephone,' answered Kiryushin.

'But perhaps you can postpone it until Monday?'

'No, it's too urgent.'

'But look—right now we are having dinner and in ten minutes my wife can come and see you.'

'No, Zhores Alexandrovich,' Kiryushin said in a rather changed voice, 'I have to speak with you. It's something too awkward to discuss with your wife.'

'That's a great pity,' I said, understanding at once that this was another trap, 'because after dinner I have to go to Moscow.'

Kiryushin now quite calmly agreed to see me on

Monday instead. My wife, however, decided that she would all the same like to go and see Kiryushin right away to find out what was so urgent. I went with her part of the way to discuss various questions which might come up when she talked to him. When I returned home after about ten or fifteen minutes, some neighbours standing near the entrance to the building told me that about three minutes after my wife and I had left the house, a small hospital bus drove up to the front entrance, and three policemen and two other men in plain clothes got out. The pair accompanied by one of the policemen entered the building but they soon came out and asked a neighbour sitting at the entrance if she knew where Medvedev had gone. The neighbour said she thought Medvedev and his wife had gone off towards the railway station. After this they all got into their ambulance and drove off.

I understood this to mean that they had decided on extreme measures. Perhaps they had now driven to the station in order to pick me up there. I had to get out of Obninsk at once—not by train, but by trying to get a lift by car to Moscow. I rushed upstairs. My two sons were busy with their own affairs. Nobody had come to knock on the door of the apartment—which meant that an agent on duty outside the building or somewhere just inside the entrance must have told the people in the bus that I had gone out. This complicated the problem. The agent must know that I had returned, and it was indeed possible that I was being followed as well. All the same I had to leave and try to shake them off. Speed was crucial, because the agent would inform them that I was back and the ambulance would return. I asked my younger son, Dima, to fetch his bicycle, catch up with his mother and tell her to come home immediately. I also told Sasha to go and stay with some friend, since we could not be absolutely certain that it was not him they were planning to take to hospital. As my son was leaving I noticed a man standing next to the window on the staircase between the second and third floors. I now packed my briefcase, wrote a short note to my wife and went to the cupboard to get my coat. At that moment I heard the sound of brakes down below at the entrance. I peeped out into the courtyard from behind the blinds and saw three policemen, Kiryushin and some other person get out of the hospital minibus. Two of the policemen stayed by it, while the others came into the building. Within a few seconds there was a knocking at the door. I at once decided not to open or respond in any way. When all is said and done, it was my right—the inviolability of the home is protected by the Constitution of the USSR. Sitting on a chair by the window, I began to observe the movements below, trying to think what I could do. The knocking at the door was repeated two or three times, rather vigorously. Then Kiryushin began to shout through the door: 'Zhores Alexandrovich. Please open the door. It's Kiryushin.'

What a swine, I thought. The agent had reported that I was back and Kiryushin thought that on hearing a familiar voice, I would rejoice and open the door. Could he conceivably believe that I still trusted him?

For a moment I thought of getting down from the balcony. I could jump on to the lawn from the second floor—it wasn't more than ten feet from the ground. But I dismissed the idea at once. There would certainly be another agent on duty on the other side of the house, and for the psychiatrists such an 'escape' would be a windfall. Kiryushin continued to shout and knock at the door.

Then he went down to the courtyard with his companions and they began to deliberate. After a short discussion all five returned. The knocking at the door began again, but with greater force. This was clearly one of the policemen. But I still made no sound. Then he began to shake the door, at first cautiously and then for all he was worth. He had clearly made up his mind to force the lock. I left the window and went into the hall; the door was already giving way, and plaster was coming off by the jamb. Then I heard Dima's voice just outside—there was the sound of a key turning, and the door opened.

'Papa, there are . . .' Dima began and stopped short, seeing my face. Behind him three policemen burst into the apartment.

'Stop,' I shouted, 'this is a private apartment.'

'It belongs to the State,' a hulking sergeant at once answered back, 'and the police have the right to enter any apartment.'

'Do you have a warrant from the Procurator? Show it to me.'

'We do not intend to arrest you. We are only accompanying the doctors.' The sergeant pointed to Kiryushin and the other man who in the meantime, without waiting for an invitation, had gone into my study and sat down seeming very much in charge of the situation. Kiryushin sat on the sofa, trying to make it clear by his whole demeanour that he was not the principal figure in all this. I sat in my chair behind the desk opposite the stranger. For a moment we looked at each other in silence. He was an undersized, rather frail-looking type, clearly someone of education. There were some kind of nervous blotches on his face, and his fingers trembled slightly. He suddenly asked me in a most affable tone, as one might ask an old friend: 'Zhores Alexandrovich, is something troubling you?'

'And who do you think you are, bursting into my apartment without permission? Surely you are familiar with the law about the inviolability of the home?'

'This apartment is not private—it belongs to the State,' the sergeant standing by the door again intervened. But the stranger motioned him to be silent.

'I am the Head Doctor of the Kaluga Psychiatric Hospital, Alexander Yefimovich Lifshits.'

'Do you have any identification or a document authorising you to do this?' I asked.

'No, but we invited you to come to the clinic, didn't we? You refused, and so we had to come to see you at home.'

'But surely you have your identity card at least?[1] How do I know that your name is Lifshits and that you are who you say you are?'

'Unfortunately I haven't got my identity card with me, but Comrade Kiryushin here, whom you know, can confirm that I really am the Head Doctor of the Kaluga Hospital.'

I asked to see Kiryushin's documents, but he didn't have them on him either.

'Since neither of you have any papers,' I said, 'then I have the right, in my own apartment, not to discuss

[1] All Soviet citizens over the age of sixteen are required to carry identity papers.

anything with you. I didn't invite you here or give you any grounds for your visit.'

'If you refuse to talk to us, then we will be obliged to draw the appropriate conclusions.' And the real, or self-styled, doctor nodded meaningfully in the direction of the policemen standing by the door. I realised that even my silence could be used as an excuse for some decision on their part. In this situation I had to restrain even my natural indignation and play for time until my wife returned.

'How is your son feeling?' asked Lifshits.

'Quite well at the moment, but surely you didn't come to me with the police because of him.'

'Why not? We might also be interested in your son's health,' answered Lifshits, and he began to ask professional questions about my son's behaviour.

'And how do you feel yourself, Zhores Alexandrovich?'

I answered that I felt marvellous.

'But if you feel so marvellous, then why do you think we have turned up here today?'

'Obviously you must answer that question yourself,' I replied.

Just then my wife ran into the room. She understood everything at a glance and began to fire indignant questions at Lifshits and Kiryushin. While Lifshits fidgeted in his chair, talking to my wife, I realised that it had not been finally decided beforehand how this unsolicited visit would end. The Head Doctor of the Kaluga Hospital had come to have a look at a man whom he had never seen before. With Kiryushin I had previously talked only about my son. They would undoubtedly have studied my medical 'history' in the local clinic—the whole affair had been in preparation for a long time—but from these papers they could only have seen that their intended victim had never consulted psychiatrists or neuropathologists, and had always been diagnosed as normal in all the yearly neuropathological checkups obligatory for people who work in medical institutes where they can be exposed to X-rays. They could have had no complaints about me from people who knew me. The doctors could come into a man's apartment without an invitation— but they could not just take a man they didn't know off to a mental hospital simply on KGB orders. Through personal observation and conversation they had to find 'evidence' and in this way 'convince themselves' that the man somebody marked down for treatment really did display signs of mental illness. For this reason it was important to talk to them only in the presence of witnesses.

I took my wife aside, calmed her and asked her to go to several colleagues who lived near by and tell them to come immediately. I gave her the name of comrades with whom I had worked at the Institute and who had medical training. While my wife did this, I continued the 'conversation' with Lifshits. Kiryushin sat silently and did not take part. At first Lifshits asked about certain aspects of my scientific work in Obninsk and earlier in Moscow. While we were talking, my colleagues from the Institute of Medical Radiology began to arrive. I invited them into the room and briefly explained the situation. The six men who came were all very solid citizens, somewhat to the embarrassment of the doctors and police. But Lifshits, quickly recovering his composure, continued the conversation. Now, however, he stopped asking irrelevant questions and came to the main point:

'Zhores Alexandrovich, in 1962 you wrote *Biology and the Cult of Personality*, an attack on Lysenko. I read it recently—it's a polemical work. But by now people have forgotten about Lysenko—the struggle in genetics is over. And instead of forgetting about it like everybody else and getting on with your work, you recently published this book abroad. Why?'

I briefly explained that whoever had supplied Lifshits with information had in fact shown him the first draft of my manuscript which had started circulating in *samizdat* in 1962 without my having anything to do with it. This version had long been outdated and I didn't even have a copy myself. By the end of 1962 I had already written another version under a different title and in considerably expanded form. In 1963 this version, called *Outline of the Controversy in Biology and Agronomy*, was again rewritten. Later I kept coming back to it, and it grew into a fully fledged history of the whole subject. I gave the book in this form to the publishing house of the Soviet Academy of Sciences, and it received a favourable response from many people. When, independently of me, it was learned that several copies of the early version had possibly found their way abroad, a special fifteen-man commission was set up on the initiative of a group of members of the Academy of Sciences to discuss the question of publication in the Soviet Union. The commission included representatives from the Lenin Agricultural Academy, the Academy of Medical Sciences (including its then president, N. Blokhin) and the Science Department of the Central Committee. It was headed by the Vice-President of the Academy of Sciences, Academician N. N. Semenov. The Institute of Scientific Information made a limited number of copies of the final version of my manuscript for the members of this commission. After careful consideration the commission unanimously recommended publication of the book in the USSR in a somewhat modified form. Academician Semenov called me in and informed me of this decision. But the proposal never came to anything. Instead, we heard that a Russian émigré journal in West Germany was intending to publish the early version of my work (the same one in fact which had obviously been shown to Lifshits). In view of this, and to protect my own interests, I gave permission to my friend Professor I. Michael Lerner, a noted American geneticist who knows Russian, to do what he had suggested to me as early as 1965. Whereupon Professor Lerner quickly translated the book, and in 1969 it was published by a serious academic publisher, the Columbia University Press. Unfortunately the publisher gave it a rather sensational title, *The Rise and Fall of T. D. Lysenko*, but the book is nevertheless a completely scholarly one. The publication of academic work abroad by Soviet scholars is not forbidden. Professor Lerner made many cuts in the text for the American edition. (I took a copy of the American edition from the shelf to show Lifshits how it looked in its final form.) I did not succeed in preventing the publication in West Germany of the earlier discarded version, but Columbia University Press exercised their right to forbid translations from the Russian version published in the émigré journal. I also sent a sharp protest to the editors of the journal in question.

This, I said, was more or less the full story of the book's publication, adding that I was ready to discuss it with any official—right up to the Procurator—if I had broken the law, but not with psychiatrists. The book had been published, and nobody had discovered anything 'psychopathological' about it—except perhaps in the mentality of some of the persons involved in the genetics controversy.

Whether or not I convinced my visitor, I don't know. He changed the subject and started talking about another book which still existed only in manuscript—the same book about international scientific co-operation which I mentioned at the very beginning of these notes.[1] At first I wasn't even sure which book he meant, because he got the title wrong and was unable to tell me what it was about. All he knew was that there was an account of the fate of Timofeev-Resovskii, or rather, about the sequel to his being awarded international scientific prizes.[2] Evidently he had been shown only this part of the book and told very little about the rest. Nevertheless he asked me why I had published this book abroad as well.

I answered that this was absolute nonsense, that someone had crudely misinformed him. After briefly describing the central theme, I said that no copies had gone abroad and that it was not even circulating in *samizdat*. If anyone thought otherwise, then let him show me facts and not indulge in fantasy. And even if it were true, I could only discuss it with a relevant official, not with psychiatrists from Kaluga.

Having reached the end of this series of questions

---

[1] *The Medvedev Papers*. See above, page 9 note.
[2] Ibid., 70–112.

obviously prepared in advance, Lifshits came to the purpose of his visit. He very politely suggested that I 'voluntarily' go with him to the Kaluga Psychiatric Hospital for a brief examination. He guaranteed that I could return home afterwards.

'But surely only if you find no signs of illness?' I asked.

'Of course,' answered Lifshits, 'but you are so sure you are perfectly well, that you have nothing to fear from an examination. If you persist in refusing a voluntary examination, it will be very much against your own interests,' he added.

I categorically rejected the idea of any psychiatric examination, remarking that since they had arrived uninvited with a detail of police, there could be no question of 'voluntary' examination, whether they tied me up and took me by force or whether I got into the ambulance on my own.

At this point my wife and colleagues joined the discussion. They started to inquire where Lifshits had got the authority to come with the police to a man whom he had never even seen before. The radiobiologists and biochemists brought along by my wife were not psychiatrists, but had nevertheless studied the basic principles of psychiatry as part of their medical training. They knew very well that someone had to instruct a psychiatrist to go to the house of a person suspected of mental illness, and that even then the psychiatrist could only act if the person had become dangerous to those around him, if he showed signs of aggression or derangement, or if he wanted to kill himself. Usually it is the relatives or colleagues who send for the doctor, or the police if he has broken the law or is guilty of a breach of the peace. But none of this applied to the present case in which so far the entire conversation had been about manuscripts.

Evading the flood of questions, Lifshits in some confusion explained that they had received 'information', that certain facts about me had come to the attention of the city and regional Party committees. Hard pressed under very professional interrogation, he finally admitted that his visit had been occasioned by a request from the Chairman of the Obninsk City Soviet, Antonenko, who had talked to me recently and found my behaviour strange. Antonenko had allegedly asked that I be examined, and now Lifshits could see for himself that it would really be best for me to agree to this. He emphasised that it was in my own interests and would only take three days. My colleagues, however, were puzzled because they knew me rather better than Antonenko, and assured him that there was no reason to have doubts about my mental health.

The conversation was now at a dead end. Almost an hour had gone by since the arrival of the psychiatrists, and the 'patient' just sat there in his chair. Something had to be done, but Lifshits clearly could not bring himself to give the ultimate order to the policemen. They all apparently very much wanted to secure the 'voluntary' agreement of the 'patient' to go to the hospital for examination. When Lifshits saw that he would not succeed in persuading me, he expressed the desire to talk to my colleagues 'confidentially'. He went into the other room and asked Kiryushin and my friends to go with him. My wife and I remained in my study under the attentive gaze of the police. The 'confidential' talks lasted almost an hour. Then one of my colleagues came to me with a 'peace proposal':

'Zhores, perhaps you should agree. Lifshits guarantees that the whole examination will not take more than three days. According to the regulations, an examination of persons hospitalised by force must be concluded strictly within three days.'

'How can he speak of "three days"? Tomorrow is Saturday, the day after Sunday,' I answered.

The 'envoy' went away but soon returned.

'He says that everything necessary will be done on Saturday and Sunday, and on Monday you will be able to return home. If you resist the police, it could turn out seriously for you.'

'I do not intend to resist the police. I'm no match for them in any case. But I will not submit to the verbal orders of the police who entered my apartment illegally. Let them use force, if they are allowed to. Besides I have absolutely no confidence in a doctor who has such a strange way of showing concern for my health, on the basis of a denunciation by the Chairman of the City Soviet. If ever I need a psychiatric examination, then I am certainly able to arrange it of my own free will, without the help of Lifshits, by going to more experienced specialists in Moscow. I feel no such need right now, and never have. I cannot even be sure that Lifshits is a doctor.'

After receiving my answer, Lifshits and Kiryushin returned to the study. Sitting down in his former place, Lifshits continued to urge me that it would be in my interests to go voluntarily to Kaluga. He tried his best to sound friendly and convincing, but sometimes there was a threatening note. I felt that he was unsure of himself, knowing full well how unwise it was to use force in front of my family and other witnesses, sharply opposed to such a procedure. It was a tricky situation.

Suddenly a police major entered the room. Where he came from, I don't know. Nobody had used my phone to call for reinforcements. None of the three policemen had left the apartment, and the major's sudden arrival was very odd. Such a high-ranking policeman would hardly be used for the enforced hospitalisation of a mental case, where nothing more than brute force was needed. Nevertheless the major immediately took command of the operation.

'What's this? Why are you refusing to submit to the requests of the doctor?' he demanded in a blustering tone.

'And who on earth might you be? I didn't invite you here,' I replied none too politely myself.

'I'm Police Major Nikolai Filipovich Nemov. I must ask you to come with me to the ambulance.'

'If you are a police major, then you must know the law about the inviolability of citizens' homes, especially as the police are responsible for law and order.'

'We are responsible for enforcement!' Nemov retorted, even thumping his chest with his fist.

'Get to your feet!' he suddenly shouted. 'I order you to get to your feet!'

Not observing any reaction to his command, the major ordered everybody to leave the room—only my wife refused. The major then made some sign to the policemen, and they rushed towards me. But my wife blocked their way and declared that she would not let them use force. Then the policemen grabbed her by the arms and dragged her into the next room. Nemov kicked the door shut. The two sergeants returned, came up to me on both sides and with a practised movement grabbed my arms at the elbow and at the wrist, twisted them behind my back and yanked me out of my chair. The one on the left did his work very painfully—the bruise lasted for a week. With my arms twisted behind my back they took me down the staircase and into the courtyard. There was already a curious crowd around their ambulance. They shoved me inside and started off.

But we didn't seem to be going in the right direction. From Red Dawn Street the ambulance turned on to Lenin Avenue instead of the main road leading to Kaluga. That meant we were heading for the Obninsk clinic, I thought with relief. But I was wrong. We did pull up at the Obninsk clinic, but only to leave Kiryushin there and allow Lifshits to transfer to the Volga in which he had evidently come from Kaluga. After this, in addition to the policemen, a nurse joined us in the ambulance, and the driver set off at full speed on the road to Kaluga.

3

The First Week of Struggle
29 May–5 June

ROY MEDVEDEV

ON Friday, 25 May, at noon, my brother rang me from Obninsk to tell me that he would be arriving in Moscow that evening with his younger son for the weekend. The boy had satisfactorily completed the sixth class, and this trip would be a reward.

I left a note for my wife and went to work. After work I had to see one of my friends, and so when I came home it was already past ten. I barely had time to take off my coat, when my wife told me that Academician Boris Lvovich Astaurov had rung to say that Zhores had been taken off to the Kaluga Psychiatric Hospital that evening. It was a complete surprise. Zhores had never told me about any of the previous attempts to subject him to a psychiatric examination; he obviously hadn't wanted to upset me. I immediately put through a call to Obninsk and spoke to Astaurov. He couldn't tell me very much for the time being, just that Zhores's wife, Rita, had rung him and said that he had been taken away by force to the Kaluga hospital. I soon managed to speak to my sister-in-law myself. Rita briefly described what had happened, and we arranged that she would wait for me the next day in the hospital grounds at about mid-afternoon.

Even though it was very late, I rang several friends of Zhores's and mine to tell them what had happened, but asked them not to do anything until my return from Kaluga. Two friends of our father, the Old Bolsheviks Ivan Pavlovich Gavrilov and Raissa Borisovna Lert, agreed to go with me to Kaluga. This was to be no more than a 'peace delegation'; we only wanted to talk to the doctors about the reasons for what had happened and try to understand the intentions of those responsible.

It was very late indeed by the time I rang the Ministry of Health of the RSFSR and then of the USSR,[1] but there was always someone on duty in these ministries at any time of day or night. However, no one could tell me anything. I asked for the telephone numbers of the persons responsible for the psychiatric section, but both ministries refused to give them and told me to ring on Monday. Clearly it was not an accident that Friday had been chosen as the day for forced hospitalisation. At the weekend most people are away from the office, many of our officials are out of town in their dachas and cannot be reached until Monday. But a great deal can happen in two days.

Despite a large dose of sleeping pills I could not get to sleep. At five in the morning I got up and typed a short appeal to friends, in which I expressed my vigorous protest against Zhores being put into a mental

[1] RSFSR is the Russian Socialist Federal Soviet Republic. Some Soviet ministries are to be found both at the federal (All-Union) and at the republican levels; other ministries and state committees (for example, the KGB) are completely centralised with no corresponding body at the republican level.

hospital and asked them to do anything each of them individually considered possible to help in his release.

In the morning I informed several close friends who were then in Moscow about what had happened. I also rang Academician A. D. Sakharov who had known Zhores since 1963 and had taken a keen interest in his writings about the problems of science. Of course everybody I spoke to on the phone was extremely indignant about the action of the Kaluga authorities and asked to be kept informed.

We left Moscow at about noon and were in Kaluga in three hours. Rita met us at the hospital. She had already seen Zhores that morning and told him we would be coming. He had been put in one of the wards of what was called the Third Wing—there were five other men besides him in the ward. The person in charge of the wing was a young woman doctor, G. Bondareva.

We went to the Head Doctor's waiting-room, but neither Lifshits nor his deputy was there. We were informed that Saturday was not a visiting day and that no one else would be admitted. But Gavrilov, Lert and Rita ignored this and went all the same to the Third Wing where the nurse on duty allowed them all into the visitors' room. At the same time I set off to look for Lifshits. One of the nurses said that I would find him in the Children's Wing. I went there and rang at the door which was opened by a duty nurse.

'I have to speak to the Head Doctor urgently.'

She slipped away, locking the door behind her, but in three minutes reappeared on the porch.

'Dr Lifshits isn't in our wing.'

Clearly Lifshits didn't want to talk to us. It must

have been reported to him that several people had arrived from Moscow. But it was absolutely essential for us to see him. I went into some office and by dialling Information was able to get Lifshits's home number. I rang and the phone was answered by a woman, apparently his wife. I explained that I had to speak with Alexander Yefimovich urgently, but that he had already left the hospital.

'Come here then, he'll be home soon.'

I noted down the address, waited for the others who were still with Zhores and then suggested that we all go to Lifshits's apartment. The working day was almost over and we thought there was a good chance of finding him at home.

In a few minutes we arrived outside Lifshits's house in Victory Square. The others remained in the car while I went up to his apartment. But he still hadn't come home. I asked whether I could wait there for him. His wife kindly invited me inside, gave me some art books to look at and then treated me to tea with home-made cakes. However I had no time to partake of all this before the bell rang in the hall.

'A comrade from Moscow has come to see you,' I heard Lifshits's wife say quietly. He walked into the sitting-room, saw me, and for a moment looked very puzzled. Zhores and I are twins, and our resemblance has misled even people who knew one of us well.

However, Lifshits quickly regained his self-control, realising his initial mistake. Yet throughout the whole conversation he was uneasy and anxious, especially as my friends rang the doorbell several times to inquire whether it wouldn't be useful for them to take part in the conversation.

Lifshits tried to assure me that psychiatrists always act only in the interests of their patients, trying to protect them from harmful emotional shocks. Many people remain quite unaware of their own mental illness and even their family and friends don't notice anything. At first everyone protests, but afterwards, after treatment, both the patients and their relatives come to the hospital to thank the doctors.

'But don't you think the very nature of the force used yesterday could have a serious effect on the mental state of Zhores, his wife and especially his children?'

'We discussed all that,' answered Lifshits, 'but we had no alternative because we were convinced that your brother would not voluntarily come to the clinic for talks with the doctors.'

Lifshits then conceded that to put a person into a ward with really ill people before the doctors' final diagnosis could not have a salutary effect on his mental state.

'Of course it would have been better if we could have put your brother in a single room until after his examination. But our hospital is overcrowded at the moment and we don't have any single rooms.'

'But what were your grounds for having doubts about my brother's mental health?'

'I read his manuscript *Biology and the Cult of Personality* and began to have doubts about the sanity of the person who had written it.'

When I asked him which particular statements in the manuscript gave rise to such misgivings, Lifshits didn't answer.

'But since this manuscript was written eight years ago,' I protested, 'it has been read by thousands of people, including a number of prominent Soviet scholars, biologists and writers. And they all spoke of it in highly favourable terms. Moreover, a year ago Zhores's book on the biological controversy was published abroad in its final form and had a great number of favourable reviews in the most reputable scientific journals. Even foreign scholars remarked that Zhores wrote it in a spirit of deep loyalty to his country, and that it could only help a return to normal in Soviet biology.'

'You are certainly entitled to your opinion, but we psychiatrists have our own views and our own criteria.'

'But what right do you have to pronounce on works outside your own field and to ignore the opinion of people much more competent than you to judge the problems dealt with in Zhores's book? Two years ago a special commission of the Academy of Sciences of the USSR discussed Zhores's book and even recommended it for publication with a few slight alterations. Do you feel yourself entitled to join in a scientific discussion in all other sciences? In physics, for example, or mathematics?'

To these questions Lifshits made no reply.

'Many people who read the recently published novels of Ivan Shevtsov,' I continued, 'feel that they are the work of a man who is mentally ill. You can see this even from what was written about them in *Yunost* and *Literary Gazette*.[1] But so far nobody has thought of subjecting Shevtsov to a psychiatric

---

[1] The novels referred to here, *In the Name of the Father and the Son* and *Love and Hatred*, published in large editions, are written in a neo-Stalinist spirit and are so grotesque and crude that they evoked protest even in some Soviet magazines such as the monthly literary *Yunost* (*Youth*) and the writers' weekly, *Literary Gazette*.

examination, although the view that he is abnormal is shared by many doctors. Moreover, if one reads Lysenko's works today or ᴋnows about his past activity, one is bound to have doubts about his mental stability as well. So why does Lysenko still attend meetings at the Academy of Sciences instead of going to a mental hospital for a psychiatric examination?'

'You talk just like your brother. I haven't read Shevtsov's novels. Perhaps Lysenko is abnormal, but he doesn't live in the Kaluga region.'

'When will the examination take place?' I asked. Lifshits replied that it would be on Sunday, and that psychiatrists would come from Moscow for it.

'But why did you choose to act on Friday and not wait until Monday? Why is the commission coming from Moscow on a weekend? Why all this rush, since it isn't a question of preventing murder or suicide, but only concerns a manuscript written eight years ago?'

'There was no particular reason—it was quite by chance that Friday was chosen as the day to bring him to the hospital.'

'Have you read Zhores's manuscript on international scientific co-operation?'

'I have some idea of what's in it.'

'What does that mean—you "have some idea"? Have you read it or not? Have you held it in your hands?'

'I have some idea of what's in it,' Lifshits repeated, and even went on to say that in this manuscript as well there were several signs of mental 'deviation'. 'As a matter of fact I have observed that your brother suffers from a split personality. He is a biologist, but is also involved with many other things which bear little relation to his immediate responsibilities. Besides, he is always dissatisfied about something, always fighting against something.'

'But then you would also have to declare Marx abnormal. He worked in a number of different fields too and was always fighting against something. No country is so perfect that a normal honest person can be satisfied with everything instead of fighting against shortcomings and things he considers to be wrong. And this is just what my brother is doing. Nearly all scholars have what you term a "split personality"—as a rule a man cannot confine himself only to his own field. If you don't accept this, you will have to put a great many people into psychiatric hospitals.'

Lifshits next tried to argue that the prolonged period Zhores had spent without working had adversely affected his mental state. It had been important for him to find employment—he had received an offer, but had turned it down.

I explained that Zhores had been illegally dismissed from the Institute of Radiology, and that for a whole year not only was no other post offered to him, but he wasn't even given the documents a scientist needs in order to apply for a new post. Only after many pleas to the President of the AMS and to the Procuracy had he received his references and been able to apply for a job at the Institute of Medical Genetics. The interviews were supposed to take place, as far as I knew, at the beginning of June.

'By what you are doing,' I continued, 'you are actually spoiling my brother's chances of getting work. Who is going to appoint a man undergoing treatment in a mental hospital?'

Lifshits assured me that he didn't know anything about the forthcoming interviews.

'If you decided to commit him to hospital, it must mean that you were acting on some provisional diagnosis. What was it and who made it?'

'Our Kaluga psychiatrist, Leznenko, observed your brother in the office of the Chairman of the Obninsk City Soviet. His diagnosis is medical and confidential.'

'But my brother and I are identical twins and we have an identical heredity. If his mental state is unbalanced although he is unaware of it, then I must be in the same condition, and it is your duty as a doctor to warn me.'

'I cannot discuss that.'

Finally I warned Lifshits that by participating in such a shameful business he was not only risking his own reputation but also discrediting the whole of Soviet psychiatry. He must think of his own future, including the possibility that in a few years nobody would want to shake hands with him.

'I realise,' I said, 'that certain individuals unknown to me are standing behind you. But when this whole venture collapses, as it most certainly will, all these other people will remain in the shadows, and you will be the only one to blame in the eyes of the world.'

After this I rejoined the others, and we drove off to Moscow. On the way Rita told us in more detail about Zhores's committal, and Lert and Gavrilov gave us an account of their conversation with him. All things considered, they found him to be quite calm. On the way we made a brief stop in Obninsk, talked to Zhores's sons, and Rita quickly got supper for us.

All the way back to Moscow I not only thought

about the steps we would have to take to get Zhores's release, but also, by going over in my mind the known facts, tried to sort out the reasons for what had happened.

I decided it would be a very good thing if on the next day somebody went to Kaluga who was so eminent that the 'commission' could not refuse to see him. Protest letters and telegrams, including some sent to the hospital, would also be invaluable.

As for the underlying motivation behind it all, there were several possibilities. It was obvious that the Obninsk authorities had played a part—Lifshits didn't attempt to conceal this. During our talk, he had several times alluded to the request of the Obninsk Party Committee and City Soviet that a check be made on Zhores's mental state. My brother had been dismissed from the Institute of Medical Radiology in March 1969 on the specific instructions of the Obninsk Party Committee, after a board appointed by it had subjected my brother to a 'loyalty check'—a procedure which did little credit to a Soviet scientific institution. After this Zhores had been unable to find work in his own field for more than a year. However, supported by his friends and family, he was able, all the same, to continue doing theoretical work in biochemistry, genetics and gerontology and keep abreast of all the latest developments in these fields. When the authorities of the Institute unofficially proposed that he 'recognise' his mistakes (in order to receive his documents), Zhores refused. All this very much irritated the local officials who apparently decided to teach this awkward scientist a lesson, hoping that it would not be lost on several others as well. But the

Obninsk authorities were not powerful enough by themselves to induce the Kaluga mental hospital to take such a radical step. The whole thing must, of course, have been co-ordinated with the Kaluga Party Committee and the Kaluga branch of the KGB.[1] A police detail with a major in charge would never otherwise have been at the disposal of a psychiatrist appearing at Zhores's apartment without an identity card or any other document. It was quite obvious that the whole operation had been carried out under the direction of some third person to whom both Lifshits and Major Nemov were subordinate. Most likely of all it was some leading official of the regional Party Committee or KGB.

However, as Lifshits told me, the commission which was to examine my brother's mental state was coming from Moscow. It was difficult to believe that a group of Moscow psychiatrists would come to Kaluga on Sunday simply at the request of the local hospital, without the knowledge of their superiors in Moscow. It was thus likely that the Kaluga authorities had co-ordinated the whole operation in general terms with someone in Moscow. But it must have been at some intermediate level. Perhaps, for example, the secretary of the Kaluga Party Committee, A. A. Kandrashenkov, had rung the Minister of Health, Petrovsky, to arrange for the confinement of my brother by these unorthodox methods.

In the eyes of the authorities even dissident intellectuals are divided into some kind of hierarchy with various categories—a 'table of ranks'. One dissident may be punished by a decision of the local authorities,

[1] That is at the regional level.

another only by the decision of the highest body. Living in the Kaluga region, Zhores found himself within the jurisdiction of the Kaluga authorities. But it was rather difficult for provincial officials to grasp the idea that there could be a total discrepancy between a person's formal status and his unofficial public standing. They didn't realise that a considerable part of the Soviet intelligentsia has a completely different system of values from those which prevail in bureaucratic circles. To me it was self-evident that many prominent Soviet scientists, writers and artists would come out in defence of Zhores, and that this affair would cause a stir abroad; but its sponsors only realised this later.

I also considered another possibility. I knew that in recent months the friends and accomplices of Lysenko, so very influential in the past, had again become extremely active. A large group of Lysenkoists had sent a letter to senior officials in which they complained about the 'persecution' of the 'Michurin school'[1] in biology. This campaign got a most sympathetic hearing at the Ministry of Agriculture and at the agricultural department of the Central Committee—and they were given some sort of promises and assurances.

One mustn't forget that all the prominent Lysenkoists, including Lysenko himself, still have powerful positions. Many of them continue to head university departments, laboratories and seed grading stations, and work in the government apparatus. Lysenko has kept all his official titles, and continues to be in charge of the famous experimental farm at Gorki.[2] But he and

[1] I. V. Michurin was a plant breeder whom the Lysenkoists regarded as their teacher.

[2] A former estate near Moscow where Lenin spent his last days. It was converted into a farm in the 1930s.

his followers no longer had their former predominance, even monopoly, in biology and agriculture—they could now be criticised in the professional journals, and their 'discoveries' are no longer greeted with such publicity and fanfares. The Lysenkoists cannot exist in these more normal conditions because their scientific bankruptcy is all too apparent, and young scientists will have nothing to do with them. This is why they decided on a counter-offensive against their opponents. Lysenko himself has often boasted to his cronies that it is 'still too early to bury him', that he would still 'show them'. When Zhores's book about him appeared in the United States, it was bitterly resented by Lysenko himself and those closest to him. He not only obtained a copy of the book but commissioned a translation from the American edition back into Russian. Even before this the Lysenkoists had been very hostile to my brother. His work on the history of the biological controversy had been written while the Lysenko school still reigned supreme. Every competent and honest biologist had known all along that Lysenko's doctrine was false and that his theory was pseudo-science. However, Lysenko and his group acquired their influence in the first instance thanks to support by administrative and Party officials, and it was only this that gave them such preponderance over other trends in biology. My brother's manuscript, circulated all over the country in *samizdat* in 1962–4, discredited the Lysenkoists not only in the eyes of young biologists, but also of scientists in other fields, writers and a significant number of officials in the Party apparatus. Even then many Lysenkoists had already tried to compromise my brother, denouncing his book as 'ideological sabotage'. On their initiative the then first secretary of the Moscow Party committee, Yegorichev, attacked Zhores and his work at a plenum of the Central Committee in the summer of 1963. Zhores became the object of a press campaign—his name was accompanied by unflattering epithets not only in the *Agricultural Gazette* and in several other journals, but also in *Pravda*. Zhores was dismissed from the Timiryazev Agricultural Academy in Moscow, and a job was found for him in Obninsk. All this came to an end only after the October plenum of the Central Committee in 1964.[1] But from the beginning of 1970 there were again ominous signs.

There could be no better bonus for Lysenko and his freinds than the accusation that Zhores was mentally unbalanced. Perhaps the Lysenkoists had used their great influence in the Agricultural Section of the Central Committee to mount the whole operation; perhaps it was they who had arranged the details with the Kaluga authorities. This supposition of mine was strengthened by the fact that the book sent to Lifshits for his 'expertise' had been Zhores's manuscript on the controversy in biology, whereas he only had 'some idea' about the other work on international scientific co-operation and was completely ignorant of everything else written by my brother. I decided to accept this supposition as a working hypothesis and act accordingly. My companions agreed with me.

We arrived in Moscow at about ten o'clock in the evening. Gavrilov and Lert got out near their homes, and I went on to Academician Astaurov, President of the All-Union Society of Geneticists. He listened to

---

[1] I.e. the fall of Khrushchev.

my account of our experiences with great attention and was in basic agreement with my conclusions. It was already too late to arrange with any other scientists for a trip to Kaluga on Sunday, so Astaurov decided to go there alone.

On the morning of 31 May I rang Academicians Sakharov,[1] Engelhardt and also several other of my own and Zhores's friends, and briefly described the situation. Many of them had already sent telegrams to different places protesting against the use of force to commit an absolutely sane man to hospital. Most of the telegrams were sent to the Ministry of Health and the Procurator-General, and often directly to the Kaluga mental hospital as well. I found out later that many of these telegrams were received by Lifshits in the hospital even before the commission met. Sakharov had sent telegrams to the Ministry of Health and to the KGB.

That same morning I went to the Soviet writers' village on the outskirts of Moscow to see Tvardovsky.[2] He knew Zhores well, was familiar with his writings and valued them very highly. Tvardovsky was thunderstruck by what I told him. Like all the others with whom I had talked that day, he was extremely indignant, immediately wrote out the text of a telegram and went himself to send it from the nearest post office. The well-known Soviet writer, V. F. Tendryakov,[3] who was Tvardovsky's neighbour in

[1] Andrei Dmitriyevich Sakharov is an extremely eminent nuclear physicist. In recent years he has become increasingly active in the Civil Rights Movement in the Soviet Union. In 1968 his book *Progress, Coexistence and Intellectual Freedom* was published in the West.

[2] Alexander Trifonovich Tvardovsky, poet and editor of the liberal magazine *Novy Mir* until 1970, when he was forced to retire.

[3] Vladimir Fyodorovich Tendryakov, novelist and short story writer.

the village, reacted in much the same way. He had met Zhores several years before when he had given a reading at the Obninsk Scientists' Club.

Tendryakov also arranged for me to see Academician P. L. Kapitsa. I had never met him before, but Tendryakov was a close friend of the family and kindly offered to take me to Kapitsa's dacha on Nikolin Hill. We got there very quickly and were greeted by Kapitsa and his guest, Academician N. N. Semenov. Kapitsa had frequently spoken up in favour of proposals for increasing international contacts between scientists and was one of the founders of, and an active participant in, the Pugwash meetings. I believe Kapitsa had met my brother several times and was acquainted with the works which had now got him into trouble. In the last few years Academician Semenov had published many brilliant pieces in the press attacking Lysenko's monopoly in biology. It was he, furthermore, who had headed the commission of fifteen scientists in 1967 which recommended the publication of Zhores's book on the biological controversy. Kapitsa was already aware in general terms of what had happened in Obninsk and Kaluga. He assured me he would do all in his power to rescue Zhores from the mental hospital.

'In my time,' he said, 'I helped get Landau[1] and several other physicists out of prison, so I have some experience in these matters. Your brother must keep calm. If you fight for the truth in science, you must be prepared for all kinds of unpleasant surprises.'

[1] L. D. Landau, eminent Soviet physicist who died in 1968. He was founder of the Kharkov Physics Laboratory for which he recruited scientists persecuted by the Nazis. In 1937 they were accused of being Nazi agents and Landau was also arrested at that time, having been compromised by his connection with them.

I replied that in any battle there should be some sort of ground rules. Our reaction had been relatively calm when Zhores was illegally dismissed from his post, and on that occasion we didn't make a fuss. Both my brother and I were prepared to answer for our actions before any court. But to put a healthy man into a madhouse broke all the rules of the game. This was such a glaring breach of the law, so scandalous, that nobody should be expected to feel prepared for it—rather, we should all be up in arms against the very possibility of such a thing.

Towards eight o'clock in the evening I returned to Moscow. I went to see V. F. Turchin, the noted physicist who had worked for a long time in Obninsk. He told me about several further moves in defence of Zhores which had been undertaken by himself and his friends B. I. Zuckerman and V. Chalidze. Late that night I met Astaurov who had just returned from Kaluga. He had arrived at the hospital while the commission was in session. He talked to Zhores immediately after the examination, and was then received by Lifshits. The chairman of the commission, who had come from Moscow, was the forensic psychiatrist Boris Vladimirovich Shostakovich of the Serbsky Institute, and he undoubtedly knew of the presence of Astaurov in the hospital. Lifshits later told Astaurov that Zhores had answered their questions 'satisfactorily'. But the commission had not decided to release him immediately. It was the opinion of the commission that although he displayed no clear symptoms of mental illness, he showed signs of 'heightened nervousness' and therefore required further observation under clinical conditions.

This was totally absurd. If a man is discovered to have no clear signs of mental illness, then what grounds could there be for keeping him in hospital? And how could you expect him to be calm if two days earlier he had suddenly been dragged out of his apartment and placed in the general ward of a mental hospital? All the same there was a certain amount of hope in the decision. One had to assume that Shostakovich knew very well what kind of verdict was expected of him by the organisers of the action. Surely the general line must have been agreed upon beforehand. Lifshits and those who stood behind him could hardly have decided to risk inviting a psychiatrist from Moscow unless he was initiated into their final plans. Yet Shostakovich had not done all that was expected of him. Something had prevented him. Was it the telegrams which had already been received at the hospital? Or the presence of Academician Astaurov? Or Zhores's answers, which even a forensic psychiatrist of Shostakovich's experience would find difficult to fault? Or was it all these factors taken together? On 30 and 31 May all major foreign radio stations and newspapers had reported Zhores's 'arrest' and committal. It was possible that Lifshits and Shostakovich didn't know about this, but the people behind them could not be unaware of the publicity which their enterprise had received. In these circumstances the 'psychiatric commission' had very likely hesitated to declare my brother unbalanced; but neither had they dared to order his immediate release. Probably Lifshits and Shostakovich had to report to someone about the new situation and receive fresh instructions. In any case we had won a little time. Whoever had been responsible for it, the plan to complete the whole operation during the weekend had been frustrated. Now we had to make good use of the time we had gained.

On Monday, 1 June, my day began with the uninterrupted ringing of the telephone. Many of our friends wanted to find out what had been decided by the commission on Sunday. I briefly described the events of the preceding day. Among those who phoned was P. I. Yakir[1] who with his friends had now actively joined in the campaign to defend Zhores. Although there had been disagreements between us in the past, they now receded into the background. We both understood that if we got Zhores out, this would help all the others who were being held in mental hospitals for political reasons. I gave Yakir a detailed description of the last three days. Many of our friends who rang told me that they had already sent telegrams; those who hadn't asked me for the address of the hospital.

At about twelve o'clock I met the well-known film director M. I. Romm, who also thought very highly of Zhores's writings. He had been out of Moscow over the weekend and knew nothing about Zhores having been put in a madhouse. I have never seen Romm so indignant and upset. He set aside all his plans for the day and went straight to the Central Telegraph Office to send cables to the Procurator-General and to the Kaluga hospital.

Of course I appealed for help not only to friends and acquaintances but also to official quarters. Returning from Kaluga late in the evening on Saturday, I had

[1] Petr Yakir, the son of a military leader shot in 1937 with others in the Tukhachevsky trial. He was himself for many years in a labour camp after his father's execution, and is now an active member of the dissident intellectual community in Moscow.

rung the inquiry department of the KGB. I was given the number of the agent on duty in the appropriate department. Explaining the gist of the matter in a few words, I asked permission to come to the KGB in order to discuss it in more detail.

'But why are you calling us and not the Ministry of Health?' the duty officer asked. His voice was cold and unfriendly.

'I have very good reason to believe that the Kaluga and Obninsk branches of the KGB are involved in this affair,' I said.

'Ring back on Monday,' he replied.

'But the commission is due to meet on Sunday. By Monday it might be too late or in any case extremely difficult to intervene.'

'Maybe, but no one will take up your case either today or tomorrow,' the KGB man assured me.

'Then whom can I turn to if your local officials choose to abuse the law on Saturday or Sunday?'

'Turn to your wife!' he answered and hung up.

I was so outraged by this rude reply, that I dialled his number again four times, but he simply didn't pick up the receiver.

During the afternoon of 1 June, I went to the reception-room of the Procurator-General. However, it proved no easy matter to get to see anyone there. The room was already full of people, most of them from out of town, who were waiting their turn to be admitted for an interview. I could not afford to lose several hours here without even being sure of a personal meeting with a responsible official in the end. Instead, as a short cut, I sent the following telegram from the nearest post office:

To Procurator-General Rudenko, Pushkin Street
15a, Moscow. Emphatically protest against forcible
putting of my brother, noted scientist and writer
Zhores Alexandrovich Medvedev into Kaluga
Psychiatric Hospital 29 May. He is absolutely well
and has never previously consulted psychiatrists or
neurologists. This action violates regulations. Commission of psychiatric experts meeting yesterday
found my brother showed no signs mental illness.
Nevertheless he is being kept in hospital in general
ward with genuinely ill patients. Demand immediate
release of my brother, inquiry into illegality,
punishment of those responsible.

R. A. Medvedev.

I also gave my return address and telephone number. I sent a similar telegram to the Minister of Health,
Petrovsky, and to the Regional Health Department
in Kaluga. Although many such telegrams were received by the Procuracy on Monday alone, neither I
nor any of my friends were subsequently invited to
come to the Procuracy, and none of the telegrams
were answered.

I met with a very different reception at the offices of
the Central Committee. One of their officials, Comrade N., listened to me attentively and took copious
notes as I talked. It turned out that many years before
he had read Zhores's manuscript on the history of the
biological controversy. He also 'had some idea' about
Zhores's work *Fruitful Meetings Between Scientists of the
World*. After speaking to someone on the phone he
assured me that nobody on the Central Committee had anything to do with the events in

Obninsk and Kaluga or, indeed, knew anything about them.

'It sometimes happens that certain officials act on their own,' N. said, and promised that all I had told him would be reported to the leadership of the Central Committee as soon as possible. As I found out later, this promise was kept and undoubtedly played a big part in subsequent developments.

But I was not to know this until later. Meanwhile we had to carry on with what we were doing. It was very late, well past midnight, when I rang Lifshits. I probably woke him up, but under the circumstances it wasn't too great an imposition on my part. After apologising for ringing so late, I asked,

'I would like to know what decision was taken by the psychiatric commission.'

'I already told your friends yesterday.'

'Why do I have to hear through friends? I'm the nearest relative and have a right to be informed officially.'

'We found that your brother shows certain signs of deviation from the norm, and we have decided to keep him for further observation.'

'You are a doctor, and you must give me an exact diagnosis. What do you mean by "deviations from the norm"? All people must deviate to some extent or other. I have certainly noticed many deviations in your behaviour, at least from the principles of Soviet ethics. Can't you give me a more exact diagnosis?'

'We haven't formulated an exact diagnosis—we have only decided to continue observation.'

'That's no answer. You are breaking the law and the regulations which you yourself said you would observe. If after three days the hospital has found no obvious sign of mental illness in my brother, he must be released at once. I warn you that otherwise I shall take legal action.'

On 2 June, in the morning, I heard about many new telegrams sent on Monday to the Minister of Health and to the Procurator-General, with copies to the Kaluga hospital. The novelist Daniel Granin,[1] who knew Zhores from many meetings in the past, sent a telegram from Leningrad. Telegrams also came from the noted Leningrad biologists V. Y. Alexandrov, V. S. Kirpichnikov and others. In Moscow, telegrams were sent by the famous writer Venyamin Kaverin, the critic B. Y. Lakshin, the writer Mark Popovsky, Old Bolsheviks S. O. Gazaryan, I. P. Gavrilov, P. B. Lert, L. M. Portnov, D. Y. Zorina and several others. Lifshits must have received a telegram every half-hour at the hospital. As I found out later, the first protest telegrams were also beginning to arrive from a number of eminent scientists abroad. The majority of them were addressed to the President of the Academy of Sciences, M. V. Keldysh.

In the afternoon of 2 June, a group of Party members of very long standing who knew my family well paid a call on the Ministry of Health of the RSFSR.[2] They were received by the head of the Department of Special Medical Aid, N. A. Demidov. After listening to his visitors, Demidov said that he knew very little about Zhores's committal to hospital—he had received a telegram from Sakharov, but hadn't spoken

---

[1] A novelist who specialises in writing about the life and problems of scientists.

[2] I.e. the Ministry of Health at the republican level, in this case of the Russian Socialist Federal Soviet Republic. See above, page 40.

to anyone at the hospital. He said that nobody at the Ministry of Health of the RSFSR had been invited in this affair. Demidov placed a call to the Kaluga Psychiatric Hospital, was connected at once and demanded an explanation from Lifshits. The explanation evidently did not satisfy Demidov and he ordered Lifshits to come to Moscow the next morning, 3 June, to give a more detailed account.

On the evening of this same day I visited Academician I. L. Knunyants who was vaguely familiar with what had happened but wanted to know more. In his time Knunyants had played a most active role in the struggle against the dominance of the Lysenko clique, and he knew Zhores well. He promised to do everything possible to secure his release. From Knunyants I went to see the writer Yuri Trifonov with whom I had become very close during the last few years. I asked him to give as much detailed information as possible to all our mutual friends, since there wasn't enough time for me to see everyone myself.

Still on Monday, one of my friends introduced me to a certain R. who promised to keep me informed about any developments involving Zhores's case at the Ministry of Health of the USSR. I very soon had reason to be convinced of the accuracy of her information. For example, on 3 June between ten and eleven, R. rang me and said that a group of eminent psychiatrists were just then meeting at the Ministry to discuss the Medvedev affair and were talking about the appointment of a new commission to go to Kaluga. She also mentioned that Lifshits had duly come to Moscow at the summons of Demidov. However Demidov had been told that this case was being handled not by his ministry (the RSFSR Ministry of Health) but at the higher level by the Ministry of Health of the USSR.[1] Apparently Lifshits was taking part in the meeting too. R. further told me that the Chief Psychiatrist of the Ministry of Health, Academician and Secretary of the AMS, A. V. Snezhnevsky, very much disapproved of the compulsory committal of Zhores. Snezhnevsky managed to talk to Lifshits at the Ministry and even supposedly told him off for his part in the affair:

'In a year's time there is going to be an international psychiatric congress in Mexico,' he said. 'How do you think this is going to make our delegation look!'

But it seemed that the Minister of Health, Petrovsky, was insisting that Zhores be kept in the hospital for an indeterminate period. This line was also taken by Zoya Nikolaevna Serebryakova, the Ministry's Chief Psychiatric Specialist at the Ministry, who was also at the meeting.

I rang the Ministry of Health and asked to speak to Serebryakova. But someone else came to the phone and said, 'Zoya Nikolaevna is at a meeting.' However I insisted that she be called to the telephone, as I wanted to speak to her about something directly related to the meeting. In a few moments Serebryakova picked up the receiver.

'I am Zhores Medvedev's brother,' I began.

'Who is Zhores Medvedev?' she interrupted me. 'I don't know any Zhores Medvedev.'

'But I believe that at this very moment you are having a meeting about him.' I began briefly to explain who in fact Zhores Medvedev was and why I

[1] See note on page 40.

was anxious about his fate. But she interrupted me before I could finish.

'And so what do you want?'

'I want your meeting to discuss the possibility of releasing my brother on my recognisances until the new commission is convened. I guarantee that Zhores will appear before it of his own free will. I know that this has been allowed in the past even in the case of people who are really ill. As you know, the first commission has not found anything wrong with my brother.'

'We no longer allow that kind of thing,' she answered.

I immediately phoned Portnov, the Old Bolshevik who had visited Demidov the day before. Briefly describing the latest events, I asked him to get hold of his friends and make another visit, but this time to the USSR Ministry of Health. I said it was most unlikely that anyone in authority would receive me that day at the Ministry, but they could scarcely refuse to see a group of Old Bolsheviks. During the talks at the Ministry he must also press for the inclusion in the new commission of one or two psychiatrists representing the family.

Portnov quickly gathered his comrades together and they got to the Ministry of Health just as the meeting was coming to an end. They were received by Serebryakova and they told her about my brother in detail. They asked her to show them the regulations relating to the procedure to be followed in cases of emergency forced hospitalisation, but she refused. She said that the new commission had already been appointed and would go to Kaluga on Friday, 5 June. My friends asked whether it was true that the family had the right to include additional psychiatrists whom they particularly trusted. Very reluctantly Serebryakova admitted that the relatives did have such a right.

'Then on behalf of the family we insist that the commission shall include psychiatrists who will be named tomorrow by Roy Medvedev.'

Serebryakova agreed to this.

When they reported this to me, I rang Serebryakova immediately. She said that the commission had already been named and that in two days there would be a new psychiatric examination.

'May I know the composition of the commission?'

'Of course: the psychiatrists G. V. Morozov, V. M. Morozov, D. Lunts, R. A. Nadzharov and A. A. Portnov.'

Several of these names were completely unfamiliar, but I had heard many unsavoury things about Lunts.

'Am I allowed to request the removal of someone from your list of doctors?' I asked.

'Yes, of course.'

'Then I emphatically wish to exclude Lunts.'

'All right, I will strike his name off. But may I ask what are your reasons for rejecting Lunts?'

'He has a very bad reputation among my friends.'

'Do you have any more questions?'

'Yes. My friends rang me and said that I have the right to ask for the inclusion of psychiatrists representing the family.'

'Yes, that is your right. But why don't you have confidence in our psychiatrists? They are very eminent specialists.'

'All the same I want to exercise my right, and tomorrow at about two o'clock I will tell you the names of the psychiatrists who will be going to Kaluga on behalf of the family.'

'Very well, but you must arrange for their journey yourself. The Ministry is not obliged to transport these people to Kaluga.'

I agreed to this.

After the conversation with Serebryakova I at once got in touch with my friends who the day before had recommended that I meet L., a psychiatrist whom they had long known to be an experienced and honest doctor.

L. was not famous in his field but he was very much in the know about the situation at the top of the psychiatric world, and could brief me on all the leading figures in it. He was extremely indignant about the use of psychiatry as a weapon of reprisal against dissent and was ready to give me all the help he could.

As soon as I met L., I felt I could trust him completely. He pointed out the obvious fact that there was really no need for a new commission. The family could express complete satisfaction with the first commission which had found no signs of mental illness in Zhores, and accordingly demand his immediate release. L. showed me a copy of the *Regulations on the Emergency Hospitalisation of Mentally Ill Persons who are a Public Danger*, and allowed me to copy down its basic points. This regulation was by no means a secret document—it was not even stamped 'Restricted'. It had a list of the kinds of cases requiring compulsory hospitalisation. Although the phrasing in places was deliberately obscure, L. assured me that nothing in my brother's work as a scientist or as a writer could even remotely qualify under any of the points on the list. It was clearly illegal to apply the present regulations to my brother's case. It had also been a violation to use the police. Their help may be sought only where the patient or his relatives put up resistance, but in the present case the police had participated from the very beginning. L. observed that as Zhores had not been brought to court, the inclusion of forensic psychiatrists on the commission was illegal. This applied to Shostakovich and even more so to G. Morozov, who was Director of the Institute of Forensic Psychiatry and should not have been put in charge of the commission dealing with Zhores's case. G. Morozov had a bad reputation in psychiatric circles. It was he who was supposed to have said, 'Why bother with political trials when we have psychiatric clinics?' Some forensic psychiatrists have military rank, and this only tends to make them more responsive to the demands of the authorities involved. Therefore it was crucial that I should request the removal not only of Lunts but of G. Morozov too. He also advised me to protest at the inclusion of Portnov, a man who was professionally untrustworthy and morally pliable. L. said that I should agree to V. M. Morozov and Nadzharov. If there was no possibility of preventing a second commission, then we should try to get it postponed for at least a week in order to make it possible to add several experienced and authoritative psychiatrists from other cities.

'We have many psychiatrists,' said L., 'who would not allow themselves to be used in any illegal action.'

And he named several psychiatrists from Leningrad, Odessa, Kharkov, Gorki, Kuibyshev, Kiev and other cities, as well as several Moscow psychiatrists who could suitably be included in the commission on behalf of the relatives. Some of them were already retired, and several, for example D. E. Melekhov, would hardly be in a fit state to make the car journey to Kaluga. But of course the commission could do its work in Moscow—it would be easier to bring Zhores here than to take a large group of psychiatrists to Kaluga.

L. and I drafted a statement incorporating all these points for the Ministry of Health, with a copy to the Procurator-General. At the end of our talk, L. told me a little about how the present situation in Soviet psychiatry had arisen. According to L., in the years 1948–1951, when various branches of science, particularly biology and medicine, were being 'taken over',[1] psychiatry was no exception. First there was the notorious 'Pavlov'[2] joint session of the Academy of Sciences and the Academy of Medical Science in 1950, which led to the systematic destruction of many promising trends in biology, physiology and medicine. This was followed by a special session of the AMS to discuss the 'position in psychiatry'. The weeding out of the 'anti-Pavlovists' from the ranks of Soviet psychiatry merged with the antisemitic campaign of 1951–2. As a result such prominent Soviet psychiatrists as Burevich, Epshtein, Shmaryant, Golant and many others were dismissed from their posts and banished from Moscow and Leningrad. Psychiatry was now monopolised by

[1] The reference is to the activities of certain cliques, supported by the Party and Stalin personally, such as the Lysenkoists in biology, who were allowed to declare their theories to be the only valid ones and purge all colleagues who did not agree.

[2] At this session the doctrines of I. P. Pavlov (1849–1936) were elevated to the status of dogma in a crude and simplified form.

the school of A. V. Snezhnevsky, who announced a new unitary 'Pavlovian theory of schizophrenia'. Subsequently Snezhnevsky, having become head of the Department of Clinical Medicine of the AMS and Chief Psychiatrist of the Ministry of Health, several times made basic changes in his comprehensive theory of schizophrenia, speaking instead of the classification of schizophrenia according to type. Snezhnevsky succeeded in foisting his much too broad classification of mental illness upon Soviet psychiatry, but it was repudiated by the World Health Organization.

Although biology and physiology, albeit belatedly, rid themselves of the consequences of the events of 1948–51, no such thing happened in psychiatry. On the contrary, it suffered even more, if anything, from the after-effects of the 'streamlining' of those years.

I did not have the time to meet personally all the psychiatrists recommended by L. My friends offered to do this for me. Only two hours later I was informed that Melekhov agreed to join the commission on behalf of the family. Snezhnevsky told my friends that he could not represent the family on the commission, but would agree to serve if he was asked to do so by the Ministry of Health. Two psychiatrists from other cities agreed to come to Moscow, but they requested a postponement until the following Sunday or Monday.

On the evening of 3 June I met Sakharov. I had already been told something about his exploit at the International Symposium on Genetics at the Institute of Genetics of the Academy of Sciences. Now he told me about it himself in greater detail. Sakharov had not limited himself to sending a few telegrams. Like me, he had seen and talked to a great number of friends and acquaintances in order to inform them about what had happened, stir them to action against the abuse of psychiatry for political purposes, and in particular to come out in defence of Zhores. A collective letter to the highest authorities was signed by Academicians Sakharov, Tamm, Leontovich, Altshuler and Dvorkin, and by Turchin, Chalidze, Zuckerman, Golfand, Kovalev and other scientists—twenty people in all. When he heard that an international symposium on genetics was taking place, Sakharov went there and getting up on the platform just as the participants had taken their seats but before the Chairman had appeared, he wrote on the blackboard in large letters:

ACADEMICIAN A. D. SAKHAROV IS IN THE AUDITORIUM COLLECTING SIGNATURES FOR A PROTEST AGAINST THE COMMITTAL OF ZHORES MEDVEDEV TO A MENTAL HOSPITAL.

The participants at the symposium, including the foreigners present, already knew about what had happened to Zhores and had been discussing it in the lobby on the previous days. They surrounded Sakharov when he came down from the platform and he had a 'good talk' with them, many of whom wished to add their signatures to the protest, but as they were young geneticists who could have got into trouble as a result, Sakharov persuaded them to refrain for the time being. A woman delegate from Romania began to say that 'such things can happen in any country'. Sakharov retorted that in any country such things should be resisted at all cost. A Soviet geneticist who gave his name as Akifyev began to assure Sakharov that Zhores Medvedev was a chronic alcoholic and had been taken to hospital in a state of delirium tremens. This, he said, was common knowledge among the biologists and only Sakharov didn't seem to know. It was difficult to imagine who this hastily improvised attempt at misinformation was intended for. Perhaps for the foreigners present? Sakharov knew Zhores well enough himself to dismiss this grotesque lie out of hand. After a little while, two men in plain clothes came up to Sakharov and asked for his identity papers. 'I didn't have them with me and I had to leave,' Sakharov said, finishing his story.

Several of my friends argued that Sakharov's behaviour was a mistake, that such an open display could only harm Zhores. But I disagreed. I believed that each person taking part in the struggle had the right to decide for himself how he must act. It would have been wrong to demand from others that they behave as Sakharov did. But it would also have been wrong to ask Sakharov to behave like anyone else. I was grateful to all my friends and Zhores's for sending telegrams, for simply telephoning various officials, for helping me with transport or for material help to Zhores's family. As for Sahkarov's action, it could not of course harm Zhores. Furthermore, it revealed the depth of indignation among scientists at one of their completely sane colleagues being thrown into a madhouse for political reasons.

On the morning of 4 June I decided to make several copies of the notorious regulations on the emergency hospitalisation of mentally ill persons who are a public danger. I wanted to show the text to several friends, and also to Zhores himself. Here is the text:

In a number of instances the need to prevent dangerous actions by persons who are mentally ill requires their emergency hospitalisation in psychiatric institutions. In accordance with this:

1. If a mentally ill person is clearly a danger to himself or those around him, the health authorities have the right (by way of immediate psychiatric assistance) to place him in a psychiatric hospital without the consent of the ill person himself or his relatives or guardians.

2. A patient who has been committed to a psychiatric institution must be examined in the course of twenty-four hours by a special commission composed of three psychiatrists who will review the validity of the decision to commit and determine whether confinement in the hospital is necessary. The nearest relatives shall be informed about the hospitalisation.

3. The main grounds for compulsory hospitalisation are constituted by the fact of the patient being a public danger, and the criteria are the following symptoms of abnormal behaviour:

(a) Psychomotor excitation with a tendency towards aggressive action.

(b) Irregular behaviour accompanied by psychological disorder (hallucinations, delusions, a syndrome of psychological automatism, a syndrome of disordered consciousness, pathological impulsiveness) if accompanied by acute affective tension and a striving towards its active expression.

(c) A systematic syndrome of delusions with

chronic deterioration, if it results in behaviour dangerous to the public.

(*d*) A hypochondriac delusional condition, causing an irregular, aggressive attitude in the patient towards individuals, organisations or institutions.

The morbid conditions enumerated above which can undoubtedly constitute a danger to the public, may be accompanied by externally correct behaviour and dissimulation. Particular caution must be exercised when assessing the psychological condition of such persons, so as not to exaggerate the evidence indicating emergency hospitalisation; it is also important to ensure by means of timely committal the prevention of dangerous acts on the part of mentally ill persons. The grounds for compulsory hospitalisation enumerated above are not exhaustive, but only a list of the most frequently encountered morbid states which present a public danger.

4. Simple though acute alcoholic intoxication is not a ground for emergency confinement in a psychiatric hospital, nor are conditions of intoxication brought about by other narcotics or affective reactions of persons not suffering from mental illness.

5. Emergency hospitalisation is to be carried out directly by psychiatrists, but in areas where there are no psychiatric institutions, doctors belonging to the general medical service may act, in which case the patient must be taken with all speed to the nearest mental hospital.

6. In cases of emergency hospitalisation the doctor who committed the patient is obliged to give a de-

tailed account of the medical and social grounds for his decision, and at the end of his report he must state his place of work, the post he occupies, his name and the time of the order for hospitalisation.

7. In cases of necessity (if relatives or guardians of the ill person object or offer resistance), local police authorities are obliged to assist in the emergency hospitalisation of mentally ill persons, if requested to do so by the doctors as specified in paragraph 5.

8. Patients hospitalised in psychiatric institutions are to be placed in hospital wards appropriate to their mental condition and the treatment they need; patients will be subject to an obligatory re-examination (not less frequently than once a month) by a special commission composed of three psychiatrists which will review the need for further confinement in the hospital. Upon improvement of the mental condition of the patient or of the clinical picture of the illness to such an extent that the patient is no longer a danger to the public, the commission of doctors will issue an opinion on the possibility of discharging the patient. Such a patient will be discharged to the care of his family or guardians.

It was obvious that the Kaluga and Obninsk doctors had most seriously violated these regulations. Zhores was in no sense an obvious danger to those around him or to himself. As grounds for hospitalisation the doctors themselves had mentioned two manuscripts, one of which had been written eight and the other two years previously. What kind of clear danger was this? The regulations speak of the need for 'particular caution' and says that one must not 'exaggerate the evidence indicating emergency hospitalisation'. But the Kaluga and Obninsk psychiatrists had shown no caution at all. The Head Doctor of the Kaluga hospital, who had been in charge of the proceedings, had never seen Zhores before in his life. The evidence was exaggerated to such an extent that it included manuscripts and books evaluated not by competent specialists but by the psychiatrists themselves. If this is the way the grounds are interpreted, no citizen of our country can be guaranteed against being carted off to a madhouse.

However, I also had certain doubts about the substance of the regulations themselves. They had been confirmed and approved by the MVD[1] and by the Procurator in 1961. But surely emergency hospitalisation was known even before this date, and it must have been regulated by some rules or other. How did the new regulations differ from the old ones? Did the new regulations increase the powers of the psychiatrists or had they now, on the contrary, been reduced?

How was it possible, in such an important document, to state that the enumerated grounds given for emergency hospitalisation 'are not exhaustive, but only a list of the most frequently encountered morbid states which present a public danger'? This means that doctors can send a person to a madhouse on the basis of other grounds not specified in the regulations. As we all know, the courts cannot sentence a man to prison or labour camp if he has committed a misdemeanour which is not provided for in the criminal code. But doctors can commit a man and subject him to compulsory treatment for reasons not set out in any docu-

[1] Ministry of Internal Affairs.

ment. All the regulations on emergency psychiatric hospitalisation are contained on one sheet of paper! Would it really be impossible to give more comprehensive guidance, setting down *all* possible grounds known to psychiatry which indicate compulsory hospitalisation?

Finally, what is one to make of the expression, 'hypochondriac delusional condition, causing an irregular, aggressive attitude in the patient towards individuals, organisations or institutions'? A person who is mentally ill can commit suicide, he can attempt murder. But how can he be a threat to institutions and organisations? And how can the degree of this aggressiveness be established in such a way as to determine at what moment it becomes necessary to put a man in a psychiatric hospital? If somebody criticises an institution, threatens it with court proceedings, exposes irregular activities on the part of those in charge of it— what is to prevent the institution in question from bringing in psychiatrists to help it? As I found out later, it was just this point of the regulations which was used by the Kaluga hospital as a basis for the committal of my brother. I never did find out, however, exactly which institution had sought their help in order to put an end to Zhores's criticism. Perhaps it was the Lysenkoist institutions which still exist in our country? Or the Censorship Department of the Post Office?[1] Or the organisation responsible for international scientific exchanges and tourism.

On the afternoon of 4 June I had an appointment

[1] The Censorship Department of the Post Office was the subject of Medvedev's work *Secrecy of Correspondence is Guaranteed by Law*. See *The Medvedev Papers*, 293–471.

with Serebryakova at the Ministry of Health. We had
arranged to meet between two and three o'clock.
However, at about twelve R. rang me and said that
she had to see me immediately. She had very important news. We met at one o'clock at the Mayakovski
metro station and went to talk in the little garden near
the station. R. told me that the new psychiatric commission headed by G. Morozov would be going to Kaluga
not on Friday but today, Thursday. The psychiatrists
on the commission had been contacted by telephone in
the evening of 3 June and the date had been changed.
Only Portnov was unable to go. R. also told me that
the commission would apparently free Zhores, because
the whole affair had become too much of a scandal.
But I wasn't convinced. In that case, why hadn't
Serebryakova informed me? Was the hurried departure of the commission an attempt to make it impossible
for 'our' psychiatrists to participate?

I left R. and went to the Ministry of Health. Serebryakova, the Chief Psychiatric Specialist, turned out
to be a young woman, not more than thirty-five years
old. Her appearance and behaviour, however, did not
inspire confidence. After reading my now obsolete
statement composed the evening before, she told me
that the commission had already left for Kaluga at one
o'clock.

'Everything has been changed. We decided to send
the commission not on Friday, but today.'

'But why didn't you inform me? After all, we said
we would meet today and arrange for the inclusion
of a representative from the family. We talked about it
yesterday at the very end of the working day, at about
five o'clock. It appears that you were misleading me.'

'No, the new decision was taken late in the evening, long after the end of the working day.'

'Then why didn't you ring me about it?'

'I didn't know your telephone number.'

'I categorically protest against G. Morozov, who is a forensic psychiatrist. I consider this commission to be incompetent to take a decision about the fate of my brother.'

'G. Morozov has gone to Kaluga not as a forensic psychiatrist but as a Corresponding Member of the AMS. Two other most eminent psychiatrists, V. Morozov and Nadzharov, have gone with him. The Ministry has every confidence in them.'

Serebryakova tried to convince me that everything would turn out all right, that the commission would sort everything out. She even conceded that Lifshits really had violated certain points of the regulations and that he would be punished.

'We want to help you, Roy Alexandrovich. Why are you being so aggressive?'

I replied that I was simply defending my rights and those of my brother. There was nothing aggressive in my behaviour, whereas the behaviour of the psychiatrists, inclined as they were to illegal action, really was a public danger. I expressed doubt about Serebryakova's readiness to help me or my brother, because in that case why had it been necessary to act with such undue haste?

Serebryakova now tried to find out from me more about Zhores and his friendship with Solzhenitsyn. In the course of our conversation she let slip two sentences which I found very significant: 'We didn't know that your brother was such a distinguished scholar,' and 'Do you know why the Obninsk Party Committee is so hostile towards him?' This seemed to confirm my guess that the whole thing had been organised by the local authorities who had only later obtained the agreement of the Ministry of Health. In the Ministry they were now apparently embarrassed by the fact that Zhores Medvedev was rather well known, with the result that the affair had received far too much publicity for their liking. I suppose they thought it would have been quite all right to put away a scientist of lesser fame.

'Can you give me the phone numbers of the members of the commission?'

'I have left my address book at home.'

'But you remember your own telephone number?'

'What are you getting so upset about? Tomorrow morning you'll know everything.'

'But I want to know everything this evening.'

I insisted, and Serebryakova gave me her number. From her office, I went to see her immediate superior, the head of the whole preventive medicine department. I realised after talking to this woman that she knew nothing of the whole affair. Apparently Serebryakova was particularly trusted by the Minister, and he conducted this kind of business through her, over the heads of her more senior colleagues. I tried to get a meeting with the Minister himself, but this was unrealistic of me. His aide told me that Petrovsky could not see me that day or in the near future. All I could do was return home and wait for news.

At nine in the evening Rita rang me from Kaluga. She was very upset. The commission had finished its work a long time before and she had already spoken to Zhores after the session. He told her that the whole examination had lasted only about twenty minutes. Questions were fired at him so rapidly that members of the commission had no chance of hearing the answers. According to Rita, the members of the commission deliberated for a long time and then went to have supper with Lifshits. The chairman refused to meet her or tell her anything. But Lifshits came to the visitors' room and told her that Zhores would certainly be released, not that day for some reason, but on the following day in the afternoon. He refused to give any explanations or answer Rita's questions. Rita didn't believe him. She was afraid they were going to take Zhores off somewhere or do something to him, and for this reason wanted to spend the night near the hospital. I calmed her as best I could, although I wasn't feeling very calm myself. The supper in honour of distinguished guests must have been over for some time by now—they were most probably on their way back to Moscow. I put in an urgent call to Lifshits, but nobody answered the phone in his apartment. In Moscow I rang Serebryakova, but it was her husband who picked up the receiver.

'Zoya Nikolaevna is not at home,' he said, 'and she won't be back until very late.'

At eleven I got the idea of ringing the hospital directly. In a stern voice I asked to talk to the doctor on duty.

'Today you had a commission from Moscow composed of Doctors G. and V. Morozov and Nadzharov. What did this commission decide in the case of Medvedev in the Third Wing?'

'The commission has decided to keep him here for treatment.'

My heart sank. Clearly the haste with which the commission had gone to Obninsk was not to be explained by any desire on the part of the Ministry of Health to release Zhores as quickly as possible and thereby hush up the scandal. The most probable explanation seemed to be that they were trying to revise the ambiguous findings of the first commission and to strengthen their case for keeping Zhores in the madhouse.

At about midnight Yakir rang me. He said that he had been told that Zhores was already home with his family. I answered that this wasn't true and that someone must be spreading such rumours deliberately to confuse people who were keeping a watch on the whole affair.

I again rang Serebryakova. It was already midnight, but her husband answered again and said that she was still not at home. I asked him to write down my telephone number, saying that it was a very urgent matter and that (I apologised for making this suggestion) if Zoya Nikolaevna didn't want to come to the telephone I would be obliged to ring all night long.

In fifteen minutes Serebryakova rang me.

'I just came home. I was busy with other matters. What are you so upset about, Roy Alexandrovich?'

'Zhores's wife rang me from Kaluga. The examination has been over for a long time, but she has not been told what the diagnosis is and the Chairman has refused to see her. She is extremely distraught and is apparently spending the night near the hospital. This way you can really drive a person mad. And she has had to leave her two children alone in Obninsk.'

'I don't know how I can help you. We have our

procedures. If a commission is sent somewhere by the Ministry, it cannot discuss the matter with anyone until it has reported back to the Minister himself. Even I don't know what the findings are yet—and in fact the final decision will only be taken tomorrow morning at the meeting with the Minister. I expect to be there myself.'

It was absurd that the Minister, a surgeon by training, should be responsible for making a decision about the fate of my brother; but it was pointless to discuss this question with Serebryakova. I again booked a call to Lifshits and asked the operator to keep ringing until someone came to the phone. After a few minutes Lifshits picked up the receiver.

'This is Roy Medvedev. You promised my brother's wife that he would be discharged on Friday. Is this true?'

'Yes, tomorrow we are going to discharge your brother.'

'Then I will come for him tomorrow.'

'But why do you have to come from Moscow. In such cases we usually deal with the wife.'

'She'll be there as well.'

'Very well. Only don't come in the morning. I will be very busy—I have a lecture and cannot be in the hospital. Come after three o'clock.'

I apologised for ringing so late. But by this time I didn't believe one word that Lifshits said—he had been deceitful too often. That night I didn't go to bed at all.

On 5 June in the morning I left for Kaluga and it was already after three o'clock when I arrived. Rita met me at the hospital. Lifshits still wasn't there—we were told that he had gone to the Regional Health Department. Rita told me that he hadn't in fact been at a lecture in the morning—she had seen him in the hospital, and reminded him of his promise to discharge Zhores that day. But Lifshits had referred to his conversation with me the night before. 'We arranged,' said Lifshits, 'to discharge Zhores after three in the afternoon, when Roy Alexandrovich will be here.' Clearly Lifshits was stalling, expecting some sort of order from the Ministry of Health or the local authorities.

I went to his office and told the secretary that I would like to talk to the doctor in charge of the case, Bondareva. She came within a few minutes, showing obvious signs of anxiety. On the one hand, she was evidently trying to make a good impression. On the other, she was afraid of saying too much. But all the same she let the cat out of the bag. There is no point in reproducing our whole conversation. Here are parts of it:

'You think that we are not concerned about your brother. I have a huge department, but I spend ninety per cent of my time on him.'

'It would be better if you looked after the others who are genuinely ill. That's your duty and what you are paid for. You have no right to ignore the other patients and leave them without medical attention . . . You have violated the regulations: even now the family have not been informed of any grounds—either medical or social—to justify emergency committal. We still don't know the reasons for the use of force.'

'We set down the grounds in the case-history within twenty-four hours, but we are not obliged to reveal them to relatives.'

'But may I see the case-history?'

'No, it's a confidential medical document.'

'Perhaps you could at least tell me briefly which provisions of the regulations you have applied in this case—we now have a copy of them.'

'Yes, I can tell you. We acted on the basis of these sections'—and Bondareva pointed to paragraph (*d*) 'hypochondriac delusional condition', and (*c*) which is formulated in such vague and ambiguous language: 'systematic syndrome of delusions with a chronic deterioration, if it results in behaviour dangerous to the public'.

'But what individual or institution was being persecuted by my brother, in your opinion? Where was the public danger? Whom is he threatening?'

Bondareva was silent.

'What was the basis for the diagnosis? Who examined my brother before he was committed?'

'Our doctor Leznenko examined him—he sat in on the conversation between your brother and the Chairman of the Obninsk City Soviet.'

'But that was only a very short talk, mainly about getting a job. Your regulations call on doctors to exercise "particular caution", don't they? What kind of caution is it—if a twenty-minute conversation is enough for a scientist to be seized and put away in a madhouse.'

'Dr Lifshits also talked to your brother before the committal. This conversation went on for more than two hours, and he confirmed the diagnosis made by Leznenko.'

'But are you conceivably unaware of the fact that Lifshits broke into my brother's apartment with the

police before talking to him? Do you think these
are normal circumstances for a meeting between a
doctor and someone suspected of being mentally ill?'

Bondareva was silent.

'And who called in the psychiatrists in the first
place? Who invited Leznenko?'

'The first papers in the case were given to us by the
Obninsk Party Committee.'

'I believe that everything that has happened is an
outrage against medicine and psychiatry. Think of the
consequences and of your reputation. It will not be too
difficult for us to find a way of raising the question of
such actions at the International Psychiatric Congress.
There are psychiatrists who are ready to consider
everyone abnormal. Here I am talking to you, and
you might well go back to your office and write down
that I displayed heightened aggressiveness and am
therefore abnormal. And if I were completely calm,
you might write that I was depressed, that I was completely indifferent to the fate of my brother and therefore, again, abnormal. But I hope you are aware that
psychiatrists are legally answerable for placing a
healthy person in a mental hospital.'

'You are accusing us—but what about you, keeping
our Head Doctor in a constant state of tension? You
and your friends ring him at all hours practically every
night.'

'That doesn't compare with your behaviour. Be-
side, he refuses to answer the phone earlier in the
evening.'

After this talk I left the office and began to take a
walk in the grounds of the hospital, waiting for Lifshits.
Strolling in the yard near the Third Wing, I unex-

pectedly saw Zhores. It was the time when patients were allowed out for their walk. I went up to Zhores and we sat on a little bench to talk. Zhores asked why they didn't want to discharge him from the hospital. I answered that there really was very little hope of their discharging him that day and that he probably would have to be patient for one or two more weeks. I described what we had been doing and what we were now planning. I also told him about Sakharov's 'performance' at the Institute of Genetics. 'They' wouldn't be able to bear such pressure for long.

Suddenly a nurse came up to us. 'Zhores Alexandrovich, will you please come immediately to Galina Petrovna.'

'But I'm allowed to have a walk, and I've only just come out.'

The nurse went away but after a minute came running back.

'Zhores Alexandrovich, Dr Lifshits and your wife are waiting for you inside. They want to talk to you about your discharge.'

'Don't believe it,' I said to my brother, but he got up and went into the wing, where he was quickly taken back to his ward.

In fact, Lifshits finally arrived at the hospital at about five. He asked Rita to his office, but she soon came out looking acutely depressed. Taking me aside, she said quietly: 'Lifshits tells me that they must still keep him in the hospital for some time.' I saw no point in going to talk to him myself.

We now returned to Obninsk, had supper and talked to the boys. Later in the evening I went to the Naro-Fominsk district where Solzhenitsyn lives in the summer in a small house standing in its own little garden. In the last six years Zhores and Solzhenitsyn had become close friends. I had been told that Solzhenitsyn was extremely anxious and upset about Zhores and wanted to know all the details. After telling him everything I knew, we discussed my assessment of the situation so far, and what I thought about the outlook for the future. I promised to keep him informed about any important new developments.

It was already almost midnight when I got home. The only person I rang was Sakharov because he had asked me to. After listening to my brief report, he asked me several questions and finally said in a tone very unusual for him, 'Well, we shall see.' He pronounced those words very slowly.

4

Medicine Standing on its Head—30 May–5 June

ZHORES MEDVEDEV

I SLEPT badly on my first night in the Kaluga Psychiatric Hospital. They put me into a general ward for six people. It was stuffy, a small light remained on all night and the nurse on duty sat by the door just near my bed. Also it had been very late when I finally got to bed. Although we had arrived at Kaluga after ten o'clock, Lifshits was waiting for us and talked to me for another hour and a half. Then they took my blood pressure, listened to my heartbeat and took away my own clothes, replacing them with the bright striped pyjamas issued to mental patients. From a conversation I overheard between a nurse and a hospital orderly, it was clear that they had been expecting me.

In the morning I got to know my neighbours and then met the doctor in charge of my wing, Galina Petrovna Bondareva. She informed me that in about an hour I would be called before a commission.

I had been placed in a relatively quiet ward. One patient, a scientist, lay here with depressive psychosis from which he had suffered periodically during the last few years. A youth with suspected psychopathy had been sent here for observation by the draft office.

My third neighbour was in the hospital by order of the Procurator—the hospital had to determine whether he was legally responsible and could be brought to trial for a fight with the police. The fourth man was undergoing compulsory treatment for alcoholism. The fifth was considered to be the most seriously ill—a pleasant young man who had already been in the hospital without a break for eight years.

Adjusting to my new situation and preparing to face the 'commission' I began to think about the workings of the system which had brought me here. It was important for me to understand who was responsible for staging this production. The Head Doctor of a regional psychiatric hospital was a fairly important man—scores of doctors and heads of departments were subordinate to him. Someone as high up as this would normally never himself have travelled to another city to see a citizen suspected of mental illness. Antonenko had neither the authority nor the power to order Lifshits to do what he had done the day before. On the contrary, whoever had written the 'scenario' had given Antonenko only a small part to play. Pressure had also been put on Kiryushin. It must have come from the regional level in Kaluga—hence the involvement of the Department of Education, Leznenko, Lifshits and the Kaluga mental hospital. Without special instructions, the Obninsk police would never have sent a detail headed by a major to help Lifshits, who had arrived without any official documents. It was apparent that Major Nemov had been waiting to hear of a speedy conclusion to the operation, so that he could report in turn to someone higher up. But when enough time had passed for a trip to Kaluga and back, and the sergeants still hadn't returned or sent a message, he could no longer contain himself and went to see what was going on. Lifshits had hinted about some information on file in the Obninsk and Kaluga Party committee headquarters, but this was not to be taken seriously because such bodies do not keep records on persons who are not members of the Party. The fact that Lifshits had read a first draft of the work on the controversy in genetics and some excerpts from the manuscript on international scientific co-operation, pointed above all to the Kaluga offices of the KGB. It would be their function to collect and keep this kind of material relating to people living in the region. Links with foreigners and correspondence with people abroad are also matters of special interest to the KGB. The judiciary has, as we know, a legal right to send law-breakers for psychiatric examination. The KGB apparently also has this right but *without* the need to observe any legal formalities. The main reason for mounting this operation must have been my manuscript about international scientific co-operation which had no doubt found its way into my Kaluga 'dossier'—perhaps in summary, together with photocopies of extracts.

But Lifshits was not directly subordinate to the regional KGB—his hospital came under the Kaluga Health Department and eventually under a special branch of the Ministries of Health of the RSFSR and then of the USSR. During the two months of preliminary preparations, Lifshits must have co-ordinated the two sides of the operation (KGB and Ministry of Health)—most probably through the Ministry of

Health of the USSR, since the KGB is an All-Union organisation and has no autonomous system in the union republics.[1] The whole performance was obviously an attempt at psychiatric blackmail and was aimed at representing my manuscript on international co-operation as the result of mental illness, the pathological delusions of someone shown to be suffering from mania, etc. At the same time they would be able to discredit my other works in similar terms, and perhaps those of my brother for good measure, since the mental make-up of twins is generally the same.

These were my preliminary hypotheses. I was not very optimistic; a man is not seized by the police in front of his family in order to be released three days later and told that the examination has not revealed anything wrong. My wife would of course have immediately informed my brother and Moscow friends about my plight. But what could they do at the weekend, when all medical and judicial institutions are shut? By Monday the 'commission' would already have given its verdict. It was no accident that Kiryushin had rung my doorbell at five o'clock on a Friday evening.

At about 1 pm on Saturday I was asked to appear before the commission in Bondareva's office. The first person I saw in the room was the unidentified official from the Regional Department of Education with whom I had talked in the office of the Chairman of the Obninsk City Soviet. He was now sitting at a desk and smiling insolently.

[1] That is, since the KGB is a completely centralised body, it would co-ordinate with the Ministry of Health at the federal level. See page 40 note.

'Stop this masquerade,' I said, 'and tell me who you are!'

'This is the head of the Kaluga Psychiatric Clinic, Vladimir Nikolaevich Leznenko.' Lifshits introduced him. The third member of the commission was Bondareva.

'This is a preliminary commission,' said Lifshits. 'The main commission will meet tomorrow and a psychiatrist from Moscow will attend.'

They invited me to sit down and began to ask questions. But first, before answering, I wanted to know about procedure. I asked whether my wife or brother could invite a well-known psychiatrist to act as their representative on the commission, and what kind of record was being kept of the proceedings. Lifshits answered that the composition of the commission was decided by the hospital alone, and they were within their rights not to show their report to an outside doctor. Conversations with patients and those under observation were not recorded in any way. The doctor writes up his conclusions afterwards.

'May I make a note of your questions while we talk?'

'No, you may not,' was the answer.

After this the interview began—some of it reproduced here from brief notes which I made in the evening of the same day when my wife brought me pencil and paper. Fortunately it is not forbidden to possess writing materials in a mental hospital.

At first they asked questions about my research work at the Institute. Then Lifshits again began to inquire about my manuscript *Fruitful Meetings Between Scientists of the World*. Judging by his questions, Lifshits now knew more about this work than on the previous evening, but still had only read the first section which describes individual episodes. The more important second and third sections had not been shown to him. These dealt with the problems in a general way and were based on a study of factual material and existing literature.[1] They also contained specific practical recommendations for a more democratic system of international co-operation between scientists and intellectuals, and demonstrated the harm suffered by Soviet science because of its relative isolation and poor organisation of international scientific contacts. Therefore, in reply to questions such as 'What were your aims in writing this work?' I could only recommend that the doctors read the whole manuscript. I must add that neither Leznenko nor Bondareva had ever seen it or my book about Lysenko. I was fascinated by two questions relating to the first section of my book on international co-operation. 'Why did you reveal the contents of certain confidential conversations which took place when you were going through the formalities of arranging a trip abroad?' and 'Why did you write about Timofeev-Resovsky without asking his permission?' The first question referred to a talk with the Obninsk KGB who had tried to recruit me as an informer, dangling the trip before me as bait.[2] I regarded this conversation as confidential only up to the moment when they started to use threats. In answer to the second question I explained that if one writes something favourable about a person, one is scarcely

[1] Part Two: 'International Scientific Co-operation—the Facts and their Consequences'; Part Three: 'Civil Rights and Legislation on Travel Abroad and State Frontiers'. *Medvedev Papers*, 113—292.
[2] Ibid., 34 ff.

called upon to show it to him.[1] I had in fact been asked
to prepare an article on Timofeev-Resovsky for the
journal *Genetics*, and the editor never thought of showing it to him before publication. In the case of a critical
article it would be even less appropriate to show it to
the person concerned. What matters most, I said, is
that the author should never go beyond the bounds of
fact and always be able to prove the validity of what
he has written.

Next they unexpectedly asked me to tell them
about a conflict in my laboratory which resulted in two
colleagues moving to another department. This had
taken place in 1965, that is, five years previously—
Lifshits and Leznenko must have heard of it while
making preliminary inquiries about me at the Institute.
I replied that these two colleagues, who were brothers,
had wanted to submit a paper about an uncompleted
project to an international congress in Moscow. It was
still some while before the congress, and they hoped
that they would have enough time to prove the substance of their conclusions. I disapproved of this and
using my authority as head of the laboratory, prevented the submission of this unfinished research. The
brothers, instead of accepting my decision, began to
protest and assert that they already had enough material
to warrant the presentation of a paper. A commission
consisting of four other heads of laboratories was set
up to adjudicate the conflict. After checking the
laboratory records, it fully confirmed my allegation.
Thereupon the two brothers asked to be transferred to

[1] Ibid., 70-112. The author's account of Nikolai Vladimovich Timofeev-Resovsky, recognised internationally as one of the greatest Soviet
scientists, is indeed favourable.

another department—after which, incidentally, one of them was promoted from Junior to Senior Research Fellow.

Next they asked questions about how I came to write my book on the history of the controversy in genetics and particularly about its publication abroad. These questions alternated with others about my activities as a scientist and as a writer.

'Why have you turned from experimental work to theory in the last few years?'

'How did the translator get a copy of your manuscript on the controversy in genetics?'

'Do you know the translator personally? When and where did you meet him?'

'What makes you think that his attitude towards our country is friendly?'

'What can be the use of the publication of this book, when the truth has already been established?'

'What's your own view of yourself as a scientist— do you think of yourself as a great scientist, or not?'

'Do you have enemies? Friends?'

'How did you spend your time after losing your post? What did you do about finding other work?'

'What is your family life like? How do you sleep at night? What do you do before going to sleep? Do you frequently have headaches?'

'Why do you want to publish abroad your book on international scientific co-operation? Who has read it?'

'Are you the sort of person who bears grudges?'

'Why did you start to engage in "publicist" activity?' and so on.

Before they began to ask all these questions, Lifshits

assured me that doctors treat as strictly confidential all information obtained in interviews with patients.

I tried to answer all their questions calmly, except those which related to other people, such as the actual identity of people who had read my book on international co-operation. I also refused to give the names of my friends and 'enemies', particularly as I never classify people as 'enemies', certainly not as personal ones. As a general principle, I consider it to be harmful for contemporary society to divide people into friends and enemies for any reason—whether social, religious, racial, national or personal.

I answered that I sleep normally, do not suffer from headaches, had not yet completed my work on international scientific co-operation and therefore didn't intend to publish it anywhere just yet. I further told them that I do not bear grudges, consider myself an average scientist—many of my colleagues and friends who are the same age have achieved significantly more success in science than I—don't engage in 'publicist' work in the usual meaning of that term but am concerned with questions related to the history of science, scientific popularisation and the sociology of science— all of which is completely compatible with my basic profession. I had not switched from experimental to theoretical work—theoretical problems have always interested me. Without going into theoretical problems it is impossible to carry on experimental work. Since my arrival at the Institute of Medical Radiology, theoretical work began to take up more of my time for understandable reasons—in Moscow until 1962 I was only concerned with my own research. In Obninsk I became the head of a laboratory and therefore had to supervise a series of different projects. These, approximately, were my answers to the various questions.

I then made the general observation that I had not expected many of the questions they had asked. It seemed to me that they bore only a very remote relationship to psychiatry.

'Psychiatrists are interested in all aspects of human activity,' answered Lifshits.

'Psychiatry has always been a social science,' added Leznenko.

When the interview was over, I was allowed a meeting with my wife and two friends who had come to Kaluga from Moscow. My brother was with them, but he had decided first to look for Lifshits. I asked my friends to find out as soon as they could about all the legal regulations concerning compulsory hospitalisation, and the legal responsibility of doctors who abuse the procedure.

On Sunday, 31 May, I was invited to appear before the second 'commission'. Besides the three Kaluga doctors whom I already knew, this one included a distinguished-looking type who was introduced to me as Professor Boris Vladimirovich Shostakovich. When I asked, 'Where do you work?' he replied that he was from the Serbsky Institute of Forensic Psychiatry.

'To what do I owe the presence of a forensic psychiatrist?' I asked Lifshits.

'Boris Vladimirovich has come here not as a forensic psychiatrist but as a consultant on general questions at the invitation of the hospital,' Lifshits answered.

The commission then began its 'work'. Most of the questions were asked by Shostakovich and although they were now being put by another psychiatrist, they

were much the same as at the first commission, albeit
in a different order. They related mainly to the history
of the writing and publication of my book on genetics
and my manuscript on international scientific co-
operation. It became clear that Shostakovich had read
the same versions of these works as had been shown to
Lifshits. But he apparently was familiar with several
excerpts from the second and third sections as well,
about which Lifshits had known nothing the day
before. To my question as to where they had seen
these works, they preferred not to answer. Lifshits
only growled out: 'Certainly not in *samizdat*.' Then
he asked yet another 'psychiatric' question: 'At your
home you showed me your book *The Rise and Fall of
T. D. Lysenko*. I noticed that it has a photograph of
the author. How did the publisher get it?'

'The translator, Professor Lerner, is an old friend. I
have corresponded with him for almost ten years and
have sent him many different photographs by ordinary
and registered post, including ones of myself. At home
I have many photographs of Professor Lerner and
other American geneticists which he also sent me by
post. One needs nobody's permission to send personal
photographs abroad by post.'[1]

It was clear during this second interview that
Shostakovich had been briefed in advance for his role
and that consequently the strings of this puppet show
were being manipulated from Moscow. Obviously he
could not have read through two rather bulky manuscripts in Kaluga that same morning. Even a quick

[1] In *The Medvedev Papers* the author explains that other materials sent
abroad by scientists and scholars must be submitted for preliminary
censorship.

reading would require two or three days, and the psychiatrists assured me that they do not read such materials in the ordinary way, but always make a careful study of them from the special psychiatric standpoint. It was also obvious that they had been required by some external agency to put certain basic questions concerning my two books. This was why Shostakovich repeated these questions, not knowing perhaps that they had been put the day before—although of course it was possible that he just wanted to hear the answers himself and he may have been applying the usual technique of interrogators, attempting to discover discrepancies between different answers to the same question.

The Serbsky Institute of Forensic Psychiatry has long had a reputation as an institution which fulfils not only medical but also political functions. The use of psychiatry for punitive purposes at the order of some non-medical authority has become a routine practice for this institution. While the examination of a criminal lawbreaker to establish the degree of his legal 'responsibility' is known as 'psychiatric examination', the term used to disguise the same procedure in political cases is '*special* examination'.

Only recently, one or two months before my own psychiatric adventure, I had managed to read the diary of former Major-General P. G. Grigorenko, whom the Serbsky Institute sentenced to be confined in a prison-psychiatric hospital for an indefinite period. Grigorenko was arrested in Tashkent on a completely absurd charge, and there wasn't enough evidence against him for an open trial; it was therefore decided to organise a psychiatric 'trial'. However, the commission of psychiatrists in Tashkent found that Grigorenko was of completely sound mind and the decision of this commission was accepted by the Tashkent court. Then Grigorenko was taken to the Serbsky Institute in Moscow, and here a commission more experienced in political cases was appointed. It included the director of the Institute, Professor G. Morozov, and the head of the 'special examination' department, Professor Lunts. They reviewed the findings of the Tashkent psychiatrists and pronounced Grigorenko to be 'not answerable for his actions' after which, at a trial behind closed doors, Grigorenko was sentenced *in absentia* to compulsory 'treatment' in a prison-psychiatric hospital on a strict regime.[1] He has now been there for two years.[2] Yet one only has to read Grigorenko's diary to see that he is completely sane, as well as being an honest, straightforward man of courageous views. And so it could not be regarded as an accident that someone from the Serbsky Institute had been made chairman of the commission appointed to examine me in Kaluga. There was nobody at Kaluga sufficiently experienced in political matters, and they had to borrow someone from elsewhere.

My interview went on for more than an hour. Sunday was normally a visiting day at the hospital, and coming out of the office I was amazed and delighted to see Academician Astaurov with my wife and other friends. I had known him for about fifteen years, long before he had become an Academician—in the days when geneticists were denounced as idealists, reaction-

---

[1] Soviet prisons and labour camps are graded according to the severity of conditions into ordinary, hard, strict and special.

[2] General Grigorenko was sentenced in 1969.

aries and goodness knows what else. I briefly described
my 'examination' and afterwards my visitors asked to
speak to Lifshits. At first he refused to receive them or
inform them about the findings of the commission,
although under the regulations the hospital was supposed to give reasons for committal within the first
twenty-four hours. Coming out to see my visitors
instead of him, Bondareva said that Lifshits had been
forced to leave urgently for Moscow. But when it
turned out after an hour that the guests were still in
the visitors' room talking with the 'patient' and
Lifshits in fact hadn't gone anywhere, the Head Doctor
agreed to grant them an interview on a further request
from Astaurov. My wife was also present. Lifshits
refused to tell them exactly what had been decided
and did not give them the grounds for the use of force,
only vaguely hinting that there were such grounds,
that there was an accumulation of evidence, etc. My
wife and friends said that they, after all, had known
me for many years and had never noticed the slightest
trace of abnormal behaviour, but he argued with them,
alleging that only an experienced psychiatrist can
detect the 'early stages' of mental illness. However, he
tried to evade their direct questions about the reasons
for regarding me as a public danger. Judging by what
he and Bondareva said, the commission had not found
any 'acute' deviations from the norm, or psychological disturbances, but nevertheless felt it advisable
to keep me under clinical observation for several more
days. My wife, telling me all this on the same day, also
said that the Kaluga Psychiatric Hospital, the Procuracy and the Ministry of Health had all received
many telegrams from friends and colleagues protesting

against the illegal forced confinement of a sane man in hospital.

Lifshits's evasiveness about the 'diagnosis' and the time of discharge was of course understandable. To judge by what he said on the day when he came to see me at my apartment with the police, it appeared that the hospital had the 'right' to hold a man for this kind of observation for three days only. This was apparently laid down in some regulation or other. The third and last day was Monday, which meant that tomorrow morning Lifshits and Shostakovich would report their conclusions to the authors of the scenario and together with them draw up the final verdict. It was quite plain, however, that there was still not enough evidence for a diagnosis of 'severe' mental illness—hence all this talk of 'early stages', 'deviations', etc. Forced hospitalisation was certainly not applicable in such cases, otherwise it would be possible to put almost anybody in a mental home. There is no such thing as a generally agreed standard of absolute mental normality, particularly one that could be applied to intellectuals. Such things as irritability, neurasthenia, neurosis, over-strain, nervous exhaustion, hypochondria, anxiety, insomnia, agitation, absent-mindedness, eccentricity, etc.—all these were 'deviations from the norm'. It was not therefore out of the question that on Monday I would be discharged. If not, then on Tuesday my wife would protest to the Minister of Health and the Procurator-General about this violation of legal regulations and demand my immediate release.

On Monday, 1 June, I was not discharged, and on Tuesday my wife duly sent detailed protest telegrams. She had to take leave from work to come again on

Tuesday to Kaluga. Visiting days at the hospital were Tuesday, Thursday and Sunday—but with the consent of the doctors, meetings with relatives could take place on any day. I found out from my wife that there had been protests by Academicians Sakharov, Kapitsa, Engelhardt, Leontovich and also by the writers Tvardovsky, Kaverin and Lakshin. News about the affair had appeared in the foreign press and been broadcast over the radio from England, the United States and other countries with details which were not always accurate. This widespread publicity might well have a favourable effect—and not for the present case alone. It threw open for international criticism the whole system of the abuse of psychiatry as a means of political persecution and made it public knowledge. In these circumstances the higher authorities in Moscow could not dismiss my case as a local Kaluga incident and would have themselves to take ultimate responsibility.

On Thursday, 4 June, my wife came to Kaluga with a friend from Moscow who was very well versed in legal questions. They brought really important news. A group of Old Bolsheviks, a number of friends and my brother had tried to get a meeting with the Minister of Health but without success. They were, however, received in the department of the Ministry responsible for psychiatric institutions. Here they learned that since the second commission had been unable to detect acute symptoms of abnormality and had not given a clear diagnosis, its findings had not been accepted.

The Minister of Health, Petrovsky, had personally approved the appointment of a new more authoritative 'commission' which was supposed to travel to Kaluga on Friday, 5 June. Its members would be G. V. Morozov, director of the Serbsky Institute who would be chairman, Dr Lunts, head of the department for 'special examination' of that Institute, Professor A. A. Portnov, Director of the Institute of Psychiatry of the AMS, and V. M. Morozov, head of the Department of Psychiatry in the Institute for Advanced Medical Training. All these would represent the Ministry while Lifshits would represent the Kaluga hospital.

The make-up of the commission was ominous. G. Morozov and Lunts had only recently condemned Grigorenko to 'treatment' for an indefinite period, setting aside the decision of their colleagues in Tashkent. However, by this time my brother already knew more about the legal rights of relatives and therefore he demanded the exclusion of G. Morozov, Lunts and Portnov as people who had a bad reputation and did not enjoy the trust of either the relatives or friends of the 'patient'. My brother asked that Professor D. E. Melekhov be included as a psychiatrist representing the family.

My visitors also told me that the protests were continuing to come in. The Moscow friend who came with my wife had discouraging news about the possibility of taking legal action against irregular confinement in a hospital. Until 1960 there were special articles in the criminal code making psychiatrists and doctors criminally responsible for placing a man in a psychiatric hospital without adequate grounds. These provisions made it possible to turn to the courts. But in the new criminal code, adopted in 1961, they were omitted. Henceforward in cases of abuse by psychiatrists—there was no possibility of action through the courts—one could only appeal through the administrative apparatus, starting with the Regional Health Department and going right up to the top, that is, to the Ministry of Health of the USSR.

At about five o'clock, after the 'rest hour', when I was able to talk to my wife again, I was unexpectedly called to Bondareva's office. There I saw Lifshits and in addition, three venerable gentlemen whom I had never seen before. Lifshits asked me to sit down and explained that this was the new commission and they wanted to talk to me.

'But my wife just told me that it was to be on Friday,' I said, astonished.

'Yes, that's true, but we decided not to drag things out until Friday and come today instead,' answered one of the members of the 'commission'. I asked who they all were and was told: G. V. and V. M. Morozov, and R. A. Nadzharov. Needless to say, Professor Melekhov was not among them. Perhaps that is why they were in such a hurry to come on Thursday—in order to avoid the presence of an independent psychiatrist.

G. Morozov conducted the proceedings. He asked questions very rapidly, often not even waiting for the complete answer. The whole interview lasted not more than twenty-five to thirty minutes. As soon as it was over, I dictated to my wife most of the questions they had asked me. The general theme was much the same as before, but the members of this new commission from the Ministry were only familiar with my work on international scientific co-operation from some sort of summary—they had never seen the text.

Therefore the questions about this work were very general: 'What was my intention in writing it?' 'Did I have a high opinion of myself?' 'Why had I begun to write works of this kind?' 'What was more important for me—scientific work or this kind of thing?' There were other questions such as: 'Who, in your opinion, is responsible for your being here?' 'Do you think your committal to hospital is justified?' 'Who are your parents?' 'Did you frequently have disagreements with your colleagues?' 'Which of your children do you love the most?' 'How long have you been without work?' 'Have you tried to find another post?' 'At what age did you become interested in biology?' etc. I answered that I did not consider my work on international co-operation to be unscholarly. It was a scientific-sociological work, flowing directly from the difficulties I had experienced in pursuing my research. It was up to others to judge its scientific value, and all I could say myself was that it still had a somewhat amateurish character, partly in view of the difficulties in getting access to many essential statistics and other data, not to mention the foreign literature on the subject. My hope in writing the work had been to further the progress of Soviet science and to help it achieve international standards in all fields. After I left the room, the 'commission' continued sitting for almost an hour.

Afterwards Lifshits went to the visitors' room where my wife was waiting to hear the verdict, and informed her that the commission had found it possible to recommend my discharge. 'It's already too late today to make the formal arrangements—come tomorrow afternoon.'

At about nine in the evening I was telling some of my new friends in the ward about this favourable outcome when Lifshits suddenly came in. 'Tomorrow you will be discharged,' he said in front of everyone— and it was apparent that he himself was very relieved about this. He added: 'I have asked the matron to prepare your clothing.' The whole business, it seemed, would have a happy ending.

On the next day I caught sight of my wife in the hospital yard at about noon, but Lifshits still hadn't arrived. For some reason she was not allowed to visit me, and I was not given my clothes although the package containing them had already been brought in and was lying on the matron's desk. Lifshits was said to be over at the Regional Health Department. Before discharging me, he was supposed to give some final advice to my wife, and she was now sitting in the yard, waiting for his arrival. After dinner I saw through the window that my wife was no longer there— presumably because Lifshits had come. Then my brother appeared in the yard. He was walking back and forth along the path looking very angry—the long-drawn-out discharge procedure must have been getting on his nerves.

At 4.30 the inmates of the Third Wing were taken out for a walk in the small square next to the hospital building, where under the watchful eye of several orderlies it was possible to breathe a bit of fresh air. I sat on a bench on the far end and my brother came up to me there. I said that for some obscure reason I might not be discharged that day. He thought that the Minister of Health might personally have authorised my committal at the request of the Kaluga authorities and might now be reluctant to admit his mistake so quickly. Then we began to talk over what immediate steps should now be taken to change the situation.

At that moment a nurse came up to us and said that I was wanted by Bondareva. I answered that I would come as soon as I had finished talking to my brother. In a minute the nurse again returned.

'The Head Doctor has come to Galina Petrovna—and they ask you to join them immediately.'

I got up and went back inside. I thought they must want to tell me the reasons for the reversal of yesterday's decision. But for some reason I was not taken to Bondareva's office but back to the ward. After waiting for about an hour, I tried to find out what was going on. Lifshits was not in the wing. Seeing Bondareva in the corridor, I went up to her and asked why I had been called in from my walk.

'Today is not a visiting day, and you were talking to your brother,' was her reply. 'I must ask you strictly to observe the rules of the hospital.'

'But I'm supposed to be discharged today—has this been changed?'

'Tomorrow Dr Lifshits will explain everything himself,' answered Bondareva.

My wife had not left after all. She must have wanted to tell me about her conversation with Lifshits, and she had managed to get into the visitors' room, where several other patients were talking to their relatives, against the rules. Until now relatives coming from other cities had always been allowed a meeting no matter what day of the week it was. But we weren't even allowed five minutes together. I was standing in the corridor which was separated from the visitors' room by a door the upper part of which was made of glass. It was locked and guarded by a nurse with instructions not to let me through into the room. But my wife and I were able to communicate by signs. Several patients stood near me in the corridor, amazed at the absurdity of a situation quite unusual in this wing. There had never before been any problems about meetings with wives. One of the astonished bystanders was my neighbour from the ward, Sasha, the youth who had already spent eight years in the hospital. His illness was cyclical—some conflict or irritation would spark off a relapse but afterwards there was usually a period of remission when he could work and study. He was a completely reasonable and also well-read young man. Right now he was in a period of temporary recovery and he was the 'elder' of the wing and also its librarian. (During periods of extended remission such patients were usually sent home and registered at the local clinic for supportive treatment. But Sasha, now nearly eighteen, had no home to go to—his mother was also in the hospital with a similar illness, and his father had deserted them long ago and had started a new family somewhere else without sending his address. Sasha in fact had grown up in the Kaluga Psychiatric Hospital, completed the sixth class and received his identity papers there. They were trying to find a guardian for him and promised to discharge him and place him in a school. As the 'elder' of the patients' council, he openly expressed his indignation to the nurse at the door. At that moment Bondareva came by. Seeing Sasha arguing with the nurse, she said to him sternly, 'Sasha, go to the ward immediately!'

'And why can't I stay here—after all, it's a public corridor,' the boy answered.

'Sasha, go to the ward!' her tone was sharper.

'Then I resign as elder of the wing!' Sasha burst out furiously. This was insubordination, but in a psychiatric hospital the staff usually don't pay much attention to such displays. On this occasion, however, the face of the young woman grew red with fury. Although Sasha went away, in twenty minutes he was summoned to Bondareva's office. Then a strapping orderly we had never seen before arrived. Very soon I saw through the window that this orderly was taking the boy to another building—to the terrible Seventh Wing. Because of the iron bars on the windows, the Seventh Wing resembled a prison. Very severe chronic cases were kept there, patients with advanced disintegration of the personality, dangerous madmen and persons under compulsory treatment by order of the courts. Soon after this a nurse and the orderly came into the ward and began to remove from the night table and elsewhere all of Sasha's belongings, which consisted mainly of books. Earning a little money in the wing's workshop by making boxes, Sasha spent almost all of it on books, and he was especially fascinated by political literature. In the course of several years the boy had managed to collect almost the complete works of Marx and Engels.

5

The Struggle Continues
6–17 June

ROY MEDVEDEV

EARLY in the morning on 6 June I began to write a long statement of protest to the Chairman of the Council of Ministers, Kosygin. Apparently the many protests sent to the Procurator-General, Rudenko, and to the Minister of Health, Petrovsky, had been to no avail. They had not put an end to the illegal and dangerous activities of the Kaluga psychiatrists and those faceless individuals who stood behind them. The Procurator did not react in any way to all the telegrams and letters which had been sent to him—and as for Petrovsky, he had if anything protected and encouraged his subordinates in Kaluga. Therefore the protests had to be addressed to an even higher authority. It might also help if some of the protests were more widely publicised—in any case I didn't intend to keep my letter to Kosygin a secret from my friends.

It was important to ensure that Zhores was visited every day at the hospital by friends and acquaintances, including well-known scientists and writers. The Kaluga Psychiatric Hospital was not a prison hospital. It was an ordinary institution of its kind and therefore was not closed to visitors. This made it much easier to keep a wider public informed—all those people who were keenly following the case. It would soon be known to all and sundry that the friends who came to see Zhores every day found him to be perfectly sane and in excellent health. This would inevitably make some people wonder who were the madmen in this case.

That same day, Zhores's friend, the noted geneticist Neifakh, rang me and said he was going to Kaluga the following day—on Sunday, 7 June. I gave him Lifshits's home address and phone number and asked him, as I had done with everyone else, to make sure to talk to him after visiting Zhores, even if it proved necessary to go to his home.

After this the telephone kept ringing without interruption. A large number of friends, including some from other cities, wanted to know what had been happening and what I thought they could do to help. I briefly described my own impressions from visiting the hospital and my ideas about what we should do next.

Many friends, unable to get through on the phone, came round to see me at home. The wife of the well-known critic Lakshin[1] came to say that her husband was ill, but that he was very concerned about Zhores and had asked his wife to find out all the latest news. In the afternoon Tendryakov's wife came by. I told her about everything that had happened in the last few days and through her I sent a message to her husband asking him to go and see Zhores in the hospital in the coming week. I thought it possible that

[1] Vladimir Lakshin. Liberal critic who writes for *Novy Mir* and is best known for his impassioned defence of Solzhenitsyn.

Tvardovsky[1] might well go with him, as he was also very anxious about Zhores's fate (Zhores had contributed to *Novy Mir* and was one of its active supporters). I knew that Tvardovsky had many complicated problems of his own just then, some of them connected with the arrangements for his sixtieth birthday celebrations in two weeks time. But it was an exceptional situation, and Tvardovsky's active intervention could mean a great deal.

Sakharov came on 6 June in the afternoon. He wanted to show me his open letter of protest to Brezhnev. The text was as follows:

To the Central Committee of the Communist Party of the Soviet Union. To the General Secretary of the Central Committee, Comrade L. I. Brezhnev

Dear Leonid Ilych,

I am profoundly concerned about the lawless action committed by the health authorities against my friend, Zhores Alexandrovich Medvedev. On 29 May, two doctors accompanied by policemen burst into his apartment and without producing any documents showing their right to detain him, they applied force and transported him to Kaluga for psychiatric examination, where he is still confined in a general ward of the city psychiatric hospital.

This whole action was totally illegal from beginning to end. The health authorities have absolutely no evidence of the kind required by the regulations that Zhores Medvedev is mentally abnormal let alone a public danger. Zhores Medvedev is a

[1] For notes on Tendryakov and Tvardovsky, see page 53, above.

completely healthy man. He is well known among Soviet and foreign scientists for his work in the fields of gerontology, genetics and the history of biology in the Soviet Union—also for his public activities carried out strictly within the law in support of Soviet democracy and international co-operation. It is possible that Medvedev's activities have been contrary to the interests of certain people, in particular those former members of the ubiquitous clan of pseudo-scientists in Soviet biology whose provocations, blunders and wild schemes have been so damaging to our country. But Medvedev's activity, I repeat, has always been strictly within the law, and in view of most Soviet scientists, highly productive.

The action taken against Zhores Medvedev has aroused the deepest indignation within the Soviet and international scientific community—it is regarded not only as an illegal act with respect to Medvedev personally, but as a potential threat to the freedom of science and to Soviet democracy.

Psychiatric hospitals must not be used as a means of repression against undesirable persons. They must be used for one purpose only—namely, to treat patients who are really ill, while at the same time respecting all their human rights.

In the case of Medvedev, the health authorities are at this very moment resorting to tactics of subterfuge and delay (for example, they switched the date of his examination without informing the specialist approved by the family and at the same time included one rejected by them; they issue reassuring statements, make false promises and spread misleading rumours). I have learned that the relatives have been deliberately deceived and that psychological pressure and intimidation have been brought to bear on Zhores Medvedev himself.

Zhores Medvedev must be released immediately. The health authorities and the Ministry of Internal Affairs must give an explanation to the public. Those who initiated and carried out this illegal action must be severely punished.

I cannot believe that such glaring illegality can be approved of by the highest authorities.

I ask you to intervene in the case of Zhores Medvedev—in the interests of Soviet legality and democracy. Believing as a matter of principle that in a socialist democratic country it is important to keep the public informed, I consider this to be an open letter.

Yours sincerely,
A. D. Sakharov, Academician
6 June 1970

In the next days this letter was very widely circulated and soon appeared in the foreign press, which increased the stream of telegrams from scientists all over the world.

That evening Rita rang me from Obninsk. She said she had not been allowed to see Zhores because Saturday wasn't a visiting day. She had tried unsuccessfully to get permission for a meeting, but after four hours of waiting was informed of Lifshits's decision—that from now on meetings with Zhores would only be permitted on the regular visiting days. However, after dinner when a professor of botany, A. I. Atabekova, came to Kaluga, Lifshits couldn't bring himself to turn away this elderly lady who had come 110 miles to see her former student. Atabekova talked to Zhores for a long time and afterwards with Lifshits, whose explanations were muddled and who struck her as a person in a state of total confusion.

From Atabekova I learned that Zhores was now suggesting that several psychiatrists might come to Kaluga along with his friends, which would enable them to give their expert opinion. This was a brilliant idea. I immediately rang the psychiatrist L., who had given me advice the week before, and arranged for him to go to Kaluga together with Neifakh. It was of course essential that any psychiatrist personally unknown to Zhores should be accompanied by one of his friends.

Zhores also asked me to see the Chief Psychiatrist of the Ministry of Health, Academician and Secretary of the AMS, Snezhnevsky, and make him understand the extent to which such activity disgraces Soviet psychiatry in the eyes of scientists and psychiatrists all over the world. One of my friends promised to organise this meeting soon.

As usual the day ended with a long phone conversation with Rita.

On Sunday, 7 June, I finished my letter of protest to Kosygin and continued my notes for our friends about the current state of affairs. Of all the meetings and conversations that day, the most important was with R., who had obtained some very valuable information. She told me that the ministerial commission, composed of the two Morozovs and Nadzharov, which had gone to Kaluga on 4 June, really had decided in favour of releasing Zhores immediately and getting him a job. True, the commission had noted in its decision that Zhores was a 'psychopathological personality' with 'paranoid tendencies'. Nevertheless they recommended that he be discharged since their 'diagnosis' did not constitute sufficient grounds for subjecting him to confinement in a hospital and compulsory treatment. The fact is that psychiatrists make a clear-cut distinction between real mental illness, which means that a man is not responsible for his actions and must hence be placed in a mental hospital, and the various neurotic conditions which are regarded as anomalous features of a person's volitional and emotional make-up, but which do not prevent him from being conscious of his actions and fully accountable for them in legal and moral terms.

The number of different types of 'neurotics'[1] is considerably greater than the number of mentally ill people, since most neurotic conditions may be explained by faulty upbringing rather than heredity. Many neurotics do not even receive psychiatric treatment.

I understood of course that the commission's decision to describe Zhores as a 'psychopathological personality' was not only a matter of face-saving but was also dictated by political considerations. It was not only a question of protecting professional honour. If it proved impossible to declare my brother mentally ill and his work the ravings of a madman, then it was necessary at least to call him a 'neurotic'. The absurdity of the commission's decision was clear from the grounds or 'symptoms' which were mentioned

[1] The Russian word used here is 'psychopath' which, however, has an entirely different meaning in English.

by the way of supporting evidence, and later copied out for me by R. from their report. One of the 'symptoms', for instance, was stated to be 'an exaggerated opinion of himself', but it was not stated whose criteria for judging Zhores as a scientist and writer were used by the members of the commission in describing his own opinion of himself as 'exaggerated'. Perhaps they accepted the judgement of the Director of the Institute of Medical Radiology, who under the pressure of the Obninsk Party committee had dismissed Zhores from his post as head of a laboratory. But if this was the case, then any view he may have had of himself, however modest, would have seemed 'exaggerated'. Another symptom was an extremely nebulous one described as 'poor adaptation to the social environment'. Surely the number of people everywhere in the world who are ill adapted to their environment and want to improve it is much greater than those who see no need for change. To declare dissatisfaction with one's social environment as a sign of neurosis was of course the greatest absurdity. The commission also stated that Zhores's writing on scientific and general themes in the last four or five years were weaker than his previous work. But again there was no indication of what criteria they were applying to his work. They even made a point of noting as a pathological symptom the fact that Zhores showed 'excessively scrupulous' attention to detail in his general writings.

But all the same, in as much as it was a question not of mental illness but only of 'neurosis', the commission did not have the right to keep Zhores in the hospital and thus made the decision to recommend his release and the finding of work for him. Then why, in spite of the decision of the ministerial commission, had Zhores still not been discharged from the hospital, and from whom did Lifshits get a new diagnosis the next day about schizophrenia? R. simply didn't know. Only the Minister of Health himself could reverse the commission's findings. We could only speculate whether he had acted on his own initiative or on the prompting of someone else.

Late in the evening the psychiatrist L. rang me. Together with Neifakh he had talked to Zhores for two hours and then they had spoken to Lifshits.

'I can certainly tell you one thing. Your brother is absolutely sane. And Lifshits is a . . .' Here L. used several very strong expressions.

On the next day, 8 June, Neifakh gave me notes of their conversation with Lifshits. Below is a part of it:

'What treatment has been prescribed for Zhores Medvedev?'

'We are not carrying out any treatment yet.'

'Will you carry out treatment by force if Medvedev refuses it?'

'I cannot answer that question now.'

'Forced hospitalisation and compulsory confinement in a hospital are legal only in cases where the patient is dangerous to himself or to those around him. In what way is Medvedev a public danger?'

'His committal was carried out according to the regulations.'

'We know all about the regulations. How and to whom was Medvedev dangerous?'

'We have to think how to improve his health.'

'Why don't you answer the question. Is it that you

don't have the right to answer, or that you don't know what to answer?'

'I have already explained that he is ill and it is better for him to stay in the hospital.'

'Is he a danger to his neighbours? Has anybody told you they feel endangered by Medvedev's behaviour?'

'We have documents supplied by the Obninsk Party Committee.'

'In what way has Medvedev shown himself to be a danger to the Party Committee? Did he threaten someone? Was he aggressive? Can you point to something concrete in his behaviour which could be interpreted as dangerous for those around him?'

'You are grown-up people. It ought to be clear to you.'

'Do you mean by this that the Obninsk Party Committee was apprehensive of Medvedev's further activities as a "publicist"?'

'I have explained it already.'

'You mean you forcibly placed Medvedev in hospital on the instructions of the Party Committee?'

'The Party Committee supplied the necessary documents. Our psychiatrist observed Medvedev in the office of the City Soviet, and we became convinced of the need for committal.'

The conversation continued in this vein for about an hour, sometimes becoming very heated. From this exchange, as well as from previous ones, it was increasingly apparent that it was not a psychiatrist who had declared Zhores to be a public danger, but a Party organisation, and that the doctors had accepted their opinion in the matter. Moreover, it was only Zhores's work as a 'publicist' which had led the Party Committee to declare him a public danger.

Monday, 8 June, was not a visiting day and nobody was able to see Zhores.

On Tuesday, 9 June, I was phoned by Tendryakov's wife. From what she said I gathered that her husband had gone to Kaluga that day together with Tvardovsky. I was very glad about this because I attached great significance to their visit. Later Tvardovsky, with his typical frankness, said that at first he had been very reluctant to go to the mental hospital. 'But then I remembered the Biblical saying: "If not I, then who— and if not now, then when?" and I no longer hesitated.'

I was told about several new letters and telegrams sent to the highest authorities. A group of Old Bolsheviks sent a telegram to Brezhnev and Kosygin. Lert and Gavrilov also sent them a long letter in which they mentioned their own visit to the Kaluga hospital on 30 May, at which time they found Zhores to be in perfect health, in complete command of his mind and will. 'However, since then,' they said in the letter, 'there has been a systematic attempt to undermine his mental health by keeping him among people who are deranged. Medvedev has been subjected to various measures designed to upset his nervous balance, and he has been threatened with enforced "treatment". All this fills us with apprehension for the fate of a man dear to us who is also a scientist needed by his country. The very possibility of such unheard-of illegality fills us with indignation. We ask the Central Committee and the Soviet government to interfere at once in this scandalous affair, which has profoundly upset Soviet scientists, cast a shadow over our medical profession and injured the prestige of our country. We trust that Zhores Medvedev will be released at once and that those responsible for this travesty of justice will be punished.' Lakshin sent a new telegram to the Chairman of the Presidium of the Supreme Soviet, Podgorny.

On 10 June, in the afternoon, I met Tvardovsky in Moscow, and he gave me a detailed account of his trip to Kaluga. He and Tendryakov spent two hours with Zhores who, they said, was behaving with great dignity. He talked calmly and with good humour about the events of the previous ten days and about conditions in the hospital. Then they asked to see the Head Doctor, but Lifshits refused to receive them until it was almost the end of the working day, no doubt hoping to avoid the encounter altogether. But they decided to wait and in the end Lifshits had to face them.

'I kept trying to look him in the eye,' said Tvardovsky, 'but I never managed it. For the whole hour's conversation Lifshits didn't once look up at us.' Tvardovsky was struck by the contrast between the behaviour of the doctor and of his patient. No doubt in order to get rid of them as soon as possible, Lifshits told Tvardovsky and Tendryakov that Zhores would be discharged from the hospital in three days' time, that is, on 12 June. However, Tvardovsky took this information at face value and warned Lifshits that they would not wait longer than three days. 'Just bear in mind,' he said to Lifshits, 'that we haven't come here in our own name only.'

The visit of Tvardovsky and Tendryakov must have produced a great impression on Lifshits because he lifted the restrictions he had placed on Zhores on

6 June. And so when the Old Bolsheviks Gavrilov and Lert came for a second visit to Kaluga on Wednesday, they had no problem about being admitted into the visitors' room. But in contrast to previous visits, the nurse on duty carefully wrote down their names in large letters on a piece of paper and took this off somewhere before showing them to a small room next to Bondareva's office. During their talk with Zhores, the nurse remained in the room the whole time, shifting from one leg to another without leaving her post. The same thing had happened when Tvardovsky and Tendryakov were there.

Lert asked to speak with Bondareva, as the doctor in charge of the case. Below are excerpts from this conversation, as recorded in notes made the next day by Lert:

> *Lert:* . . . How is it possible for a man to be forcibly locked up without the presentation of any evidence? Particularly a man who has never had a trace of mental illness or ever needed to consult either psychiatrists or neurologists, who has never given relatives, friends or colleagues any reason to complain about his behaviour.
>
> *Bondareva:* In this kind of situation it is very difficult for psychiatrists to find a common language with relatives or other people who know nothing of the subject. It sometimes happens that a patient shows no external signs of illness and behaves like an absolutely healthy person.
>
> *L:* But really! You psychiatrists are not high priests with your own magical language that nobody else can understand. If there was no preliminary

psychiatric examination, it means that whoever declared Zhores to be ill must be just as much an ignoramus about psychiatry as I am.

B: But he was examined by a psychiatrist.

L: When and where?

B: The psychiatrist Leznenko was present when Zhores Medvedev came to talk to the Chairman of the Obninsk City Soviet.

L: And how did a psychiatrist come to be in the Chairman's office when she was having a talk with one of her constituents?

B: Well, I don't really know. Apparently someone from the City Soviet had some dealings with Medvedev, was struck by the oddness of his behaviour and called in a psychiatrist.

L: Then am I to understand that the Chairman of the City Soviet is responsible for beginning this whole affair?

B: I don't know whether it was Antonenko or somebody else who works there.

L: But as the doctor in charge of the case, I assume you know exactly what these anonymous officials from the City Soviet found so odd in Medvedev's behaviour?

B: That's a medical secret.

L: But if officials from the City Soviet can know, why is it being kept secret from Zhores's wife and brother? A patient is not told he has cancer, but his family is warned . . . By what you say, you are giving the impression that the reasons for committal are clearly not a medical secret but some other kind.

B: Our sole concern is the welfare of the patient.

L: If we are to talk about the welfare of the patient, to use your term for a moment—although Zhores is in fact perfectly well—then what was the reason for compulsory hospitalisation? As far as I know, it is not applied to all patients, but only to those who are a public danger. Perhaps you could tell me what deeds or actions of Zhores Medvedev were a threat to those around him?

B: He is mainly a danger to himself.

L: In what sense? I, for example, smoke, which endangers my own health. But as a rule this sort of thing is my own affair, as long as I am neither a drug addict nor an alcoholic—and do not become violent or harm other people. Even chronic alcoholics—who undoubtedly are a danger to themselves—are not subject to compulsory hospitalisation if they are no danger to other people. And so in what way is Zhores Medvedev dangerous?

B: It's not so much *what* he writes as certain actions which accompany this writing. He brings a certain influence to bear.

L: That means, if I understand you correctly, that it is Zhores Medvedev's *views* that constitute a danger to the public? Do you really believe that it is within the competence of medicine to decide whether particular views are harmful or beneficial?

B: We judge Medvedev's mental state only on medical evidence . . . surely you must know that we doctors bear legal responsibility for our diagnoses, and if only for that reason we try not to make hasty judgements.

L: Should bear legal responsibility—but unfortunately that is not always the case. But one thing is
certain: you will have to live with your conscience for ever—it will be impossible to hide
from your conscience and nobody else's authority
can save you . . .

On the next day, Thursday, 11 June, Zhores's
Moscow friend B. I. Zuckerman was able to see and
talk to him. He also spent some time with Lifshits,
who was again rather clumsy in dodging questions and
trying to extricate himself.

I learned a very important piece of news that day.
The Minister of Health, Petrovsky (though himself a
member of the Academy, he had until now blankly
refused to meet his colleagues who had been trying to
get an interview with him), had now called a special
meeting for twelve o'clock on Friday and had invited
to it Academicians Sakharov, Kapitsa, Alexandrov,
Astaurov and Semenov. The President of the Academy
of Sciences, Keldysh, would also be present. From the
Ministry there would be Snezhnevsky and G. Morozov.
This was, therefore, to be a rather representative
gathering—three of the participants being members of
the Central Committee. However, the agenda did not
inspire much hope, because the telegrams sent to the
prospective participants invited them to discuss the
'case of Zhores Medvedev's illness'.

On that same Thursday I was informed that if
Zhores's stay in the hospital dragged on, there would
possibly be sharp protests at the International Symposium on Biochemistry which was to begin in Riga
on 21 June (with the participation of seven Nobel

Prize winners) and also at the International Congress of Historians in Moscow which would be in August. Some foreign scientists believed that Zhores had been put in a mental hospital as a reprisal for the publication of his book on the genetic controversy in the United States. When I told Sakharov about all these latest developments, he said he had heard from Keldysh about the setting up of a government commission at a very high level to deal with the Medvedev affair. It was probably this that had prompted Petrovsky to call a meeting with the group of Academicians who had been actively concerned about my brother's fate.

On the evening of 11 June, together with one of my friends, I tried to see the Head Psychiatrist of the Ministry of Health, Snezhnevsky, suggesting a private meeting in his apartment. However, he refused to see me, on the grounds that under the circumstances it could be regarded as an attempt to put pressure on a doctor before an important conference. But he was willing to receive my friend. During their conversation, Snezhnevsky said he had no reason to doubt the findings of the ministerial commission of 4 June that Zhores Medvedev was a 'psychopathic personality' with an 'exaggerated opinion of himself'. However Snezhnevsky recognised that such a diagnosis did not in any way call for compulsory hospitalisation and confinement in the hospital, and therefore Zhores must immediately be released and work found for him. But he must also be registered in a psychiatric outpatient department and undergo check-ups from time to time. Then Snezhnevsky began a discourse to the effect that illness, *including* mental illness, is no disgrace and does not infringe on a person's rights, etc.

My friend objected that none of Zhores's relatives or friends could agree with the 'diagnosis'. The circumstances in which the 'examination' had taken place precluded a calm and objective appraisal of the medical facts. Of course mental illness was not a disgrace, although it did tend substantially to restrict a person's rights. However, the intolerable thing was the deliberate description of a healthy man as mentally ill or 'psychopathic'. How could the ministerial commission have arrived at such a subtle diagnosis in no more than twenty or thirty minutes? My friend absolutely denied that Zhores had 'an exaggerated opinion of himself', although he remarked that such a view was characteristic of a great many scientists, writers, actors, etc.

On Friday, 12 June, the famous Soviet writer Venyamin Kaverin[1] rang me. He said he and his wife were going to Kaluga that day. Kaverin knew Zhores very well. The next day he told me he had had a long and very good talk with Zhores, and had left a letter in the hospital for Lifshits who was out of town.

On the same day I heard from Sakharov about the meeting at the Ministry of Health (from the beginning Sakharov warned the others that he did not consider the proceedings to be confidential and would not feel obliged to keep silent about what was said).

The first to speak was Snezhnevsky. He gave something in the nature of a lecture on the achievements of Soviet psychiatry and its high scientific standards. As proof he read out several testimonials by foreign scientists on the state of Soviet psychiatry. He also

---

[1] Venyamin Alexandrovich Kaverin, veteran Soviet novelist. Some of his stories written after Stalin's death deal with the persecution of scientists.

talked about the plan to create in the Soviet Union a large contemporary psychiatric centre which would have at its disposal all the latest achievements in the field. Snezhnevsky admitted that there were isolated psychiatrists here and there in the provinces whose methods were still medieval, which meant that occasional mistakes could occur. Without going into the substance of the 'Medvedev case', he went on to say that if the Kaluga psychiatrists had erred in some way, then the Ministry of Health had enough power and adequate means to correct their mistake without the interference of 'outsiders'. However, several writers and scientists had launched a whole campaign apropos of this one incident, thereby damaging the reputation of Soviet psychiatry as a whole. Thousands of people, suffering from mental disturbances, would be afraid to turn to psychiatrists, as a result of which their health would be gravely jeopardised. In other words, Snezhnevsky was accusing the Academicians and writers concerned of inhumanity. Enumerating the various kinds of mental illness which demand hospitalisation, Snezhnevsky spoke of 'obsessive reformist delusions', and at this point he shot a penetrating professional glance at Sakharov. 'I found it comic,' Sakharov commented, 'but of course I know it's not very funny for people who land up in a mental hospital after being diagnosed like that.'

Next G. Morozov spoke. He told the assembled Academicians about the already notorious 'diagnosis' of 'paranoid tendencies' and listed the symptoms we have already mentioned earlier. He added, however, that given such a diagnosis, the hospital should discharge Medvedev subject to outpatient supervision.

But there had been so much hullabaloo about this whole affair, that if Medvedev were released at once, his opinion of himself would go up even more and his condition would only deteriorate. Thus Morozov also made accusations of inhumanity, but now in regard to Zhores.

The Minister of Health, Petrovsky, said that the discharge of a patient was entirely the affair of the hospital, and the Ministry did not interfere in such matters. 'It could be that right now, while we are talking here, Medvedev has already been discharged from the hospital.' Then he urged all those present to cease their campaign on Medvedev's behalf and allow the Ministry to sort things out. He also slipped in a reproach to Sakharov for 'unpatriotic behaviour' and somebody even recalled what Pavlov had once said about an earlier case of violation of the law: 'This is our own Russian shit, and we will sort it out ourselves without any help from abroad.'

In the subsequent discussion, Sakharov, Astaurov and Kapitsa, who all knew Zhores personally, tore the Ministry's 'diagnosis' to shreds and showed how ridiculous the list of 'symptoms' was. Then Sakharov said that the Academicians present at this meeting had no control over Soviet, let alone international, public opinion, and that protests against the compulsory hospitalisation of Zhores Medvedev would come to an end only after he was free. Sakharov categorically rejected all accusations of 'inhumanity' and lack of patriotism and went on to speak of the statements that might well be made by foreign delegates to forthcoming international scientific conventions.

'Our authorities know how to deal with such

things,' Petrovsky answered, although it was far from clear how any Soviet 'authorities' could prevent foreigners from speaking out.

The meeting at the Ministry of Health went on for about three hours, and Petrovsky left looking very glum. Obviously he had not succeeded in achieving his own purposes, or those of certain other people either.

As later events showed, this meeting was a serious turning point for Petrovsky; he realised that it was time to yield and gave orders along these lines to Lifshits.

It was already after midnight when I phoned Lifshits in Kaluga. He had promised Tvardovsky to release Zhores in three days' time, and the time was now up. I wanted to ask him, therefore, whether he intended to keep his promise. Answering the telephone and listening to my question, Lifshits said that the hospital would release Zhores on Wednesday, 17 June.

'But first you promised me to release my brother on 5 June, then you promised our friends it would be 9 June, then you told Tvardovsky that you would discharge him on 12 June, now you talk of 17 June. What reason have I to believe you this time?'

On Saturday, 13 June, Zhores's friend from Moscow, Chalidze, went to Obninsk—he was very well informed in legal matters. Chalidze helped Rita draw up an application in the proper legal terms, in which she demanded that Zhores be released in the care of his family. The *Regulations on Psychiatric Hospitals* of which Chalidze had a copy permitted this kind of discharge, and hospitals were usually glad to agree because of the shortage of beds. If the hospital refused the request of the family, then it had to be officially set down in writing. However, Lifshits, on being presented with this application by Rita and Chalidze, turned it down, repeating that Zhores would be released on Wednesday, 17 June. They asked the obvious question: What was the point of waiting until Wednesday? If the discharge had in fact been decided upon, why not on Saturday or Sunday, or if necessary even on Monday? But Lifshits didn't answer.

On Sunday, 14 June, Zhores had an unusually large number of visitors at the hospital. The physicists V. F. Turchin and A. G. Vasiliev came, as well as several other friends and acquaintances. But on that day there were no talks with the doctors.

On Sunday afternoon Solzhenitsyn rang me. He asked me to meet him at one of the squares not far from the Sokol metro station. He said he had waited for two weeks, but now couldn't wait any longer, and felt that he simply had to speak out in defence of Zhores and all the other persons held in psychiatric institutions for political reasons. But he was worried about whether his intervention could possibly harm Zhores and therefore wanted to talk it over with me. I gave Solzhenitsyn all the latest news and told him about the meeting at the Ministry of Health. Now Lifshits was promising to release Zhores on Wednesday, but we had no faith in his promises and intended to carry on just as before, putting maximum pressure on the doctors and those who stood behind them. It was possible that all these promises about an imminent discharge were being made for the express purpose of confusing the public and weakening its sense of indignation. Therefore I felt that Solzhenitsyn's intervention could in no way do any harm and had no objections whatsoever.

Early in the morning on 15 June, one of our mutual friends brought me Solzhenitsyn's letter, which by the end of the day had become widely known not only among the Moscow intelligentsia at large, but also abroad. The text was as follows:

THIS IS HOW WE LIVE:

Without any arrest warrant or any medical justification, four policemen and two doctors arrive at the home of a healthy man. The doctors declare that he is mad, the police major shouts: 'We are the agency of enforcement! Get to your feet!' They twist his arms behind his back and take him off to the madhouse.

This could happen tomorrow to anyone of us, and it has just happened to Zhores Medvedev, a geneticist and publicist, a man with a brilliant, subtle and precise mind and a warm heart (I have personal knowledge of his disinterested help to sick people dying in obscurity). Because of the very *diversity* of his talents, he is charged with being abnormal, a 'split personality'. His very sensitivity to injustice, to stupidity, is presented as a 'morbid deviation', 'poor adaptation to the social environment'. Apparently, to harbour thoughts other than those which are *prescribed* means that you are abnormal. Well-adjusted people all think alike. And there is no means of redress. Even the appeals of our best scientists and writers are to no avail—it is like talking to a blank wall.

If only this were the first case! But it has become

fashionable, this way of settling accounts—with no pretence at seeking out guilt, when it is too shameful to state the real reason. Some of the victims are well known, others remain obscure. Servile psychiatrists, who break their Hippocratic oath and are able to describe concern for social problems as 'mental illness', can declare a man insane for being too passionate or for being too calm, for the brightness of his talents or for his lack of them.

Yet simple prudence should teach restraint. After all, no one so much as laid a finger on Chaadaev,[1] but we have been cursing his persecutors for over a century. It is time to understand that the imprisonment of sane persons in madhouses because they have minds of their own is *spiritual murder*, a variation on the *gas chambers* and even more cruel: the condemned suffer torments more fruitful and prolonged. Like the gas chambers, these crimes will *never* be forgotten, and those involved will be condemned for all time, during their life and after their death, without benefit of moratorium.

In lawlessness and evil-doing one must always remember the boundary line beyond which man becomes a cannibal.

It is a very limited calculation to think it possible to live relying only on force, continually disregarding the protest of conscience.

A. Solzhenitsyn
15 June 1970

I don't remember whether any of our friends went

[1] Petr Yakovlevich Chaadaev (1794–1856), the philosopher officially declared mad on the order of Nicholas I in 1836. See below, pages 181–2, 196–7.

to Kaluga on Tuesday, 16 June. But Rita was there almost the whole day and Lifshits again repeated his promise that the discharge would be on Wednesday, refusing even to discuss the possibility of it happening right away. One had the impression that a decision was imminent that same day and that Lifshits was again stalling. Perhaps the meeting of the high-level commission mentioned by Keldysh to Sakharov was scheduled for that very Tuesday.

6

Psychiatric Blackmail 6–17 June

ZHORES MEDVEDEV

On the morning of 6 June it became clear that the 'liberal' period was over and that Lifshits had received new instructions the day before from both Kaluga and Moscow.

After Sasha had been transferred to another wing, the same thing happened to two other patients whom I had got to know well—like me they were in the hospital for political reasons. One of them, a young man of about twenty-four, soon after demobilisation from the army had begun to write memoranda to different official bodies sharply criticising the Komsomol[1] for having degenerated into a bureaucratic organisation. He had proposed the creation of a new, more democratic youth association. I never read any of these memoranda, but practically everyone is familar with the bureaucratic ways of the Komsomol. All the same, a proposal to reorganise it had obviously been taken for the 'reformist delusion' of a madman. The second person, a middle-aged man, was picked up on the street early one morning for sticking up a declaration that he had composed himself. In these

[1] The Youth Organisation of the Soviet Communist Party.

handwritten declarations, he criticised the Kaluga Party Committee on whose orders he had been sacked, three months previously, from the local school where he taught. After several hopeless attempts to be reinstated or find a new job, he exercised his constitutional right of freedom of speech to complain about this arbitrary treatment. And here he was in the hospital with a condition diagnosed chiefly as 'poor adaptation to the conditions of the social environment'. Both 'patients' had been undergoing intensive treatment for three months already. The man who had proposed the reorganisation of the Komsomol received periodic insulin shock. The author of the declaration had been prescribed something milder—two powerful depressant drugs which according to the doctors would change the 'basic structure' of the psyche.

Curtains had been pinned over the glass door between the corridor and the visitors' room. The right to walk in the grounds adjacent to the non-violent Third Wing was withdrawn. Now we were all taken for exercise to the small 'pen' fenced off from the rest of the hospital grounds by a high enclosure with doors that could be locked. Patients from all parts of the hospital gathered here. In the Third Wing it was called 'the cage' and patients went there unwillingly. I was warned that visits would be allowed only on the appointed days (and for not more than fifteen or twenty minutes), and that it was desirable if only relatives came. All my letters had to be handed unsealed to the matron who then apparently passed them on to the doctors for 'medical censorship'. To judge by all this, it looked as if they were preparing a long stay for me in the Kaluga hospital.

Even assuming that my short interview with the commission had been recorded either in writing or on tape (which was very unlikely) I doubt very much whether it would reveal any grounds for diagnosing my condition as 'severe' or 'dangerous to the public'. Although the commission had been headed by a forensic psychiatrist who was fairly experienced in producing the right kind of diagnoses, both he and his colleagues could not fail to understand that the abuse of psychiatry, so easily carried out in the conditions of a prison-psychiatric hospital (where a man is cut off from the outside world and can only be visited by close relatives once every six months), was not at all easy in a normal mental hospital where friends and relatives could visit a patient three times a week, spending sufficient time with him to convince themselves that he was not in fact out of his mind. In such a situation, blatant falsification was scarcely feasible, while a subtler approach with talk about 'slight deviations', 'early stages' or 'neurosis', etc., didn't get them anywhere—such diagnoses are not a proper basis for forcible hospitalisation and compulsory 'treatment' against the will of the relatives and the 'patient' himself. What is more, all the members of the commission stressed that they had no doubts about my capacities for professional work in biochemistry, gerontology or genetics, thus implying that I should be given a post in my special field. To keep me in hospital without treatment made no sense at all, but at the same time the commission could not bring itself, understandably, to recommend treatment with depressant drugs or shock. The members of the ministerial commission must undoubtedly have been aware already of the numerous protests, foreign press reports and radio broadcasts, and they would scarcely wish to figure as the chief actors in the spectacle. But of course they hadn't been sent to Kaluga with such urgency merely to see to my discharge. The hospital itself had the power to do this. It could be arranged by Lifshits, or even by Bondareva who usually decided the fate of the patients in her wing without any interference from the Head Doctor—this despite the fact that most of them were rather more serious cases from a medical point of view. The third commission was undoubtedly sent in order to delay the discharge, and to lend its authority to the local doctors who were clearly ill-equipped to face such strong external pressures. But this commission also disappointed the hopes placed in it in certain quarters. Its decision, which resulted in my being told on Thursday about my impending release, had evidently not been accepted in these quarters—and the whole performance was beginning all over again.

On Saturday, 6 June, I was examined by a neuropathologist. In response to his commands I closed my eyes and touched the tip of my nose with the index finger of each hand in turn, distinguished between the sharp and blunt ends of a scalpel lightly applied to my skin, did not react to being tickled but did react to the blows of a hammer on my knee. Besides this I was given an encephalogram, the results of which were never shown either to me or to my wife. On Saturday I had another long talk with Lifshits and Bondareva. They started by questioning me on my family background. This was very indicative—it meant that they were trying to find evidence of schizophrenia, which may be hereditary in origin. I described the lives of all my nearest maternal and paternal relatives and what they did for a living—grandfathers, grandmothers, cousins, nieces and nephews. Happily, none of them had ever been in need of psychiatric treatment nor were there any cases of nervous disorder. All the male and female adults had led a normal working life in their various professions.

Leafing through some papers, Lifshits suddenly asked: 'But when you were talking to the psychiatrist about your son, you said that a sister of his grandmother had been treated in a psychiatric hospital. How was she related to you?' I explained that this was in fact a sister of my mother-in-law and that we were not blood relations. (I found out later she was in fact not even my mother-in-law's sister but her cousin.) Lifshits's questions showed that he had been ordered to dig out anything he could and that they were going through all the records at their disposal with a fine comb. This was borne out by the questions put by my 'psychiatrists' in a further talk on the evening of 6 June.

'When you worked at the Institute, why did you write to people abroad on Institute stationery?' asked Lifshits, inquiring about something that was hardly within his sphere. The question showed that Lifshits had himself seen or been told about 'evidence' gathered by the 'commission' which in the spring of 1969 looked into my 'ideological background' and my correspondence with people abroad, examining letters that had been intercepted. My dismissal from work was recommended by this illegal commission and took effect the day after it met.

I explained to Lifshits that I had used Institute stationery only for official correspondence about spare parts for laboratory equipment, chemical reagents, etc. The head of a laboratory has every right to do this. I never used official stationery for personal correspondence with friends.

'And why didn't you observe the regulations about official correspondence, which you signed when they were shown to you?'—another psychiatric question. Only the official in charge of the 'Special Section'[1] of the Institute could know that I had signed the regulations, always marked 'secret', on the rules for corresponding with people abroad. In other words, Lifshits had also talked to him. Again I had to explain that these regulations had been shown to me only shortly before the meeting of the 'ideological commission' described above and my subsequent dismissal. They were of no direct concern to me since they applied only to people working on classified research projects. Therefore I had signed them not as a pledge to observe them but only to indicate that I had read them. Although I was not supposed to divulge the contents of these secret regulations, neither was I obliged to observe the rules laid down in them.

'How did Solzhenitsyn's troubles begin?' Bondareva asked out of the blue.

'What does that have to do with me?' I protested.

'But really now, I wasn't asking as a doctor. I was just curious.' She was embarrassed.

'Is it true that your first scientific writing was called *On the Essence of Life*?' asked Lifshits.

By this question he involuntarily betrayed the

[1] The department responsible for 'security'.

conversation (no doubt 'confidential') which he must have had with a friend of mine from student days who was now working at the Institute of Medical Radiology. Only he knew about the existence of this work and what its title was. It was actually not a learned work but a paper given at a student scientific conference in 1945. At that time I was a first-year student at the Timiryazev Agricultural Academy and had indeed delivered a short lecture on this theme. It was a discussion of Engels's proposition that 'life is the form of existence of albuminous bodies and consists in their constant self-renewal'. In the collection of essays from this conference published two years later, my work appeared under a completely different title and only one other participant could possibly have remembered the original one. I later learned that this was the case and that on 5 or 6 June Lifshits had indeed come to Obninsk to collect material. He had even asked my next-door neighbour whether there were scenes in my household, whether we quarrelled and shouted at each other. There was no doubt about it: my doctors had really been very busy, stopping at nothing to unearth any oddities in my character and behaviour almost from birth.

From then on I had talks with them like this almost every day. There were the usual questions about gerontology, my scientific interests and my way of life—whether, for example, I like to plan things in advance, what sort of food I preferred, etc. And then they would suddenly slip in questions which had no bearing on my mental health.

'Do you keep copies of letters you have posted abroad?' Bondareva asked casually. 'And where do

you keep them? Do you think that all letters sent
abroad are examined by the post office?'

I already had a fair idea of Bondareva's intellectual
level and remembered her saying that she didn't read
foreign books; I had no doubt that someone had put
her up to these questions. She probably didn't even
know that mail for abroad is handled by a special
department of the post office in Moscow.

On the evening of 8 June, Lifshits spent a long time
trying to convince me that to engage in 'publicist'
writing in addition to one's normal professional work,
scientific or other, was a sign of a 'split' or 'dis-
associated' personality, an obvious symptom of illness. 'In time, of course, the hospital will discharge
you,' he said, 'but you must completely stop all this
other activity and concentrate on experimental work.
If you continue your publicist activities, then you will
inevitably end up back here with us.' Lifshits repeated
this 'prognosis' many times in different guises. I tried
to argue with him about it, giving many examples of
scientists who were engaged in journalist, literary or
political activities, without anyone holding it against
them. The majority of Soviet writers had other
occupations before they became professional literary
men (they include some former scientists), but nobody
put this kind of transformation down to mental illness. It is normal, not pathological, to have a variety
of interests. Psychiatrists must not draw conclusions
from the direction of a person's creative activity—
there is no rule against having several professions,
especially with so much more leisure time available
these days. One can only seek clues to pathological
symptoms in the results of a person's creative activity.

Works written by someone who is really mentally ill would be illogical, contrary to the facts, just a conglomeration of disconnected ideas.

'Look,' I proposed to Lifshits, 'let's take that manuscript which worries you most of all' (meaning my book on international co-operation) 'and go through it systematically, picking out all the obvious nonsense, the groundless assertions, the incoherent or obsessional ideas. Do you think this is what we shall find?'

At this proposal Lifshits began to explain confusedly that the problem was a more subtle one, and it was not just a question of whether the text was comprehensible or not. The author's ideas might make sense and be consistent, he might be completely in control of his intellect, but he could still be ill-adapted to the environment. The author could be 'fighting windmills', ignoring the real facts of his situation, so that his propositions were divorced from reality.

Lifshits also tried to make my wife understand this concept of 'poor adaptation to the social environment'. In one of their conversations, he said, according to my wife's notes, 'poor adaptation to concrete circumstances—this is the main symptom. Another person with his intellect would be able in time to adjust and adapt—this is the normal thing—but Zhores Alexandrovich is unable to do this. He just forges ahead, ignoring the real situation.'

On Sunday, 7 June, my friend from Moscow, the noted biologist A. Neifakh, came and brought along a psychiatrist who pretended to be a biologist also. (According to the new rules drawn up only for my benefit, the nurse on duty had to report the names of all my prospective visitors to Lifshits or Bondareva and permit a meeting only with their consent. These meetings then took place in a special room and only in the presence of the nurse. Any exchange of parcels in either direction had to be done through her.) After spending time with me, my visitors asked to talk to the Head Doctor, who agreed to receive them even though it was Sunday. On this same day I was able to see the text of the Regulations of the Ministry of Health, of 10 October 1961, on the *Emergency Hospitalisation of Mentally Ill Persons who are a Public Danger*. In these regulations, after some extremely vague and very generalised formulations giving the grounds for hospitalisation, there are two additional points which can be interpreted so broadly that the doctors are entitled to commit any person to a mental hospital if the authorities so desire.

The morbid conditions enumerated above which can undoubtedly constitute a danger to the public, may be accompanied by externally correct behaviour and dissimulation . . .

The grounds for compulsory hospitalisation enumerated above are not exhaustive but only a list of the most frequently encountered morbid states which present a public danger.

The psychiatrists are thus given very wide scope to invent new syndromes requiring forcible hospitalisation, or for declaring that supposedly 'normal' citizens are in fact really mentally ill persons simulating normality. The celebrated revolutionary Kamo,[1] ar-

---

[1] Kamo (Semyon Arshakovich Ter-Petrosyan, 1882–1922). In 1907, under Stalin's supervision, he organised bank robberies in Tiflis and Kutais.

rested for his role in the so-called 'expropriations' (the term for bank robberies in which guards and employees were frequently killed), successfully simulated madness for several years in order to avoid the death penalty. What our psychiatrists now seem to be suggesting is that people suffering from severe mental illness can successfully simulate normality for many years in order to avoid the madhouse.

Psychiatry is an extremely complex and many-sided field which by now has a vast body of knowledge at its disposal. However, in the regulations the most important section defining the conditions and circumstances for compulsory hospitalisation takes up no more than one page of the typewritten text. But mentally ill persons dangerous to the public were committed, often against their own will or the wishes of their families even before 1961, when the Ministry of Health issued the present regulations. This indeed has long been the practice, everywhere in the world. The procedure is provided for both in law and in the medical code and has always been carefully regulated. So what was the point of issuing the new regulations? According to the accompanying note from the Minister of Health, these regulations had been agreed with the Ministry of Internal Affairs (this in order to make it possible for psychiatrists to get help from the police), with the Ministry of Justice (hence the removal from the legal code of the provision concerning the criminal responsibility of psychiatrists for wrongful committal) and with the KGB. The new regulations simplify and facilitate the procedure for putting people in a mental hospital. In other countries what was done to me, for example, could happen only after the conflicting views of the psychiatrist (in my case Leznenko's) and of the hospitalised person and his family or guardians had been submitted to the arbitration of some legal body, generally a court of law. This guards against abuse and prevents confinement in mental hospitals being used simply as a substitute for imprisonment. The new regulations exempt the doctors from any legal supervision, and rely only on the principle of faith in the doctor's discretion; but in the Soviet Union, medicine is entirely subordinate to the state.

The regulations also provide for compulsory treatment, which seems rather superfluous since it is obvious that once a man is in the hospital, he must be treated. But Lifshits was clearly flouting the regulations on this point—ten days had gone by since I had been given emergency psychiatric 'aid', but no 'treatment' had yet been prescribed. Realising the absurdity of hospitalisation without treatment, on 8 June Lifshits rather cautiously asked me how I would react if he prescribed a course of drug treatment with two powerful depressants. I replied that I would feel exactly the same about this as I had felt about the experiments which Hitler's doctors carried out on prisoners of war in the concentration camps. When Lifshits proposed something similar to my wife, her answer was in the same vein.

When a patient refuses the prescribed treatment, the doctors have the right to treat him by force, administering the appropriate drugs by injection. But the doctors of the Kaluga hospital shrank from going this far—they were by now under enough pressure from outside public opinion as it was without asking for more. Apparently the consultants who had been brought in were also unwilling to recommend compulsory treatment.

Lifshits and the other authorities continued to receive telegrams and protest letters and Lifshits, at least, was being badly shaken by them. As we found out later, he passed on copies of all letters and telegrams to the Kaluga Party Committee and perhaps to some other body as well. These authorities somehow got the idea that the majority of the telegrams were bogus— that either my brother alone or with someone else's help had sent all these telegrams to Kaluga, signing the names of famous scientists, writers and other members of the world of culture. In one of our regular conversations, Lifshits in the presence of Bondareva questioned the authenticity of some of the telegrams.

'These people can hardly all know you personally, yet they all categorically contradict the opinion of the doctors, claiming to have known you for many years. The person who makes up these telegrams is obviously going a bit too far. I suppose your brother is behind it all.'

I replied that I hadn't in fact seen the telegrams but the suggestion that some of them might be fake was absolutely absurd. If he thought that these telegrams were not genuine, I could ask my wife to bring my address book and Lifshits could then ring the senders, either from home or from the hospital, and speak to them personally.

On Tuesday, 9 June, Tvardovsky and Tendryakov came to visit me. After we had talked for a long time, they asked to speak with Lifshits. My wife was also present at their conversation. The talk ranged over many questions and could hardly have brought much satisfaction to Lifshits who was very nervous and never looked up from his desk. The two writers contended that if a certain Comrade X has been known for many years to dozens of scientists and other intellectuals who have read his works, heard lectures by him and talked with him informally without ever noticing the slightest signs of mental illness or any other 'deviations from the norm', then it evidently means that there are none: mental illness, after all, shows itself mainly in a person's behaviour with others and in his works.

Lifshits tried to argue that mental illness can be detected only by a trained psychiatrist. He didn't seem to realise that the editor of an important magazine—Tvardovsky has been editor of *Novy Mir* for fourteen years—is constantly getting manuscripts and letters written by mentally disturbed people, schizophrenics, paranoiacs, graphomanics, etc. An experienced editor does not attempt a medical diagnosis, but he is quicker than any doctor to distinguish a 'sick' work from a 'sane' one, though 'sick' ones do occasionally slip into print through an editorial oversight. (The literary experts have never found such things in *Novy Mir*[1] but they are not unknown in *October*.[2])

However, the Kaluga doctors were deeply affected by their conversation with Tvardovsky and Tendryakov. Lifshits morally surrendered to them and this

[1] *Novy Mir* (New World), liberal monthly, until 1970 when its editor, Tvardovsky, was forced to resign.

[2] *October*, a literary monthly magazine, edited by Kochetov and associated with the neo-Stalinists.

was soon apparent from the improved behaviour of the hospital staff towards me. Restrictions on visits were relaxed and walks were again allowed in the grounds next to the wing. Lifshits promised the two writers that he would discharge me that same week —that is before 13 June—and he was evidently quite sincere. When all was said and done, the commissions sent from Moscow and all the other outside bodies were only peripheral factors—my actual treatment, including my discharge, could only be the responsibility of the Kaluga doctors, and it was they who bore the brunt of the pressure from both sides. This pressure was all rather too much for them and the final outcome of the struggle was not clear-cut.

To judge by conversations with the doctors between 6 and 11 June, the original intention had been to keep me in hospital for 'treatment' for several months. After this, I was to be registered as an outpatient in Obninsk, or sent to Kaluga once a month for a checkup. Without this further plan, my forcible committal was utterly pointless, and would have been shown up for the criminal abuse it was. The preliminary diagnosis of 'severe mental illness dangerous to the public' had clearly been supplied before 29 May, on the basis of the 'evidence' presented by the Party committee and the opinion of Leznenko. But in agreeing to take on the chief parts in the scenario, Lifshits, Leznenko and Bondareva never imagined that they would be called upon to give so many explanations and clarifications, and have to talk to so many people. They were well aware that all these conversations were afterwards immediately put down on paper and then discussed with others—but there was no avoiding them. Their most difficult problem was having to explain exactly in what way I was a public danger.

On 12 June, in the afternoon, the day on which Lifshits had promised Tvardovsky that my discharge would take place, the Minister of Health, Petrovsky, called a special meeting to talk with representatives of the scientific community who had been protesting. I heard about this meeting the next day.

The arguments with participants at the meeting very much irritated the Minister of Health. All the same it proved to be the occasion for some kind of decision—on 12 June in the evening Lifshits told me that my discharge was now set for 17 June.

'But you have already said you would discharge me several times before. Why should I suppose that this new date is any more reliable?' I asked.

'This time we will most definitely discharge you,' was the answer. But I didn't have a great deal of faith.

On 12 June in the afternoon, Kaverin and his wife came to see me. But Lifshits was not in the hospital at the time, and Kaverin couldn't speak to him.

On 16 June Lifshits set a time for a last meeting with my wife, in order to give her some final advice. It amounted to urging her that in the interests of the family she must use her influence to get me to stop spending my time on 'sociology' and 'publicist activity'. He confirmed that on the next day she could come for me.

On 17 June my wife came to Kaluga on the first train. Neither Lifshits nor Bondareva were there— they arrived at about nine o'clock. Before being allowed to change into my own clothes I also had to listen to some final advice from the doctors. Both of them assured me that they were only concerned about my health, that the interests of the patient were supreme. All along Lifshits had been trying to convince me that I must stop my 'publicist activities', but now he made a special point of asking me not to write any account of my stay in the Kaluga hospital. He told my wife that the Party Committee had given instructions for my immediate reinstatement at the Institute of Medical Radiology and even named the laboratory in which I would be given the post of senior research fellow.

'If you continue to act along previous lines and don't put an end to your publicist activities, we doctors will be unable to help you.' And Lifshits shrugged, hinting that in those circumstances the affair would be taken up by other authorities.

With these parting words I was released from the hospital, to freedom.

7

The First Days after Zhores's Release

ROY MEDVEDEV

On 17 June at about eleven in the morning, the telephone rang in my apartment—it was Zhores from Kaluga. He had at last been released and was going home to Obninsk. He would spend the first day with his family and come to Moscow on the 18th in the afternoon.

And so, our struggle had come to a successful conclusion, above all thanks to public opinion, whose representatives had taken such strenuous and unanimous action against this outrage. I immediately, of course, began to ring our friends to tell them the wonderful news.

When I rang Romm,[1] his wife said that half an hour before he had been summoned to the District Party Committee to attend some meeting about Zhores's case. My first thought was that they had called Romm in to tell him about Zhores's release. But when we met later in the evening so that I could thank him for his support, I learned with astonishment that he had

[1] Mikhail Romm, a leading film producer. See above, page 57.

in fact been summoned for 'criticism' and that the session had been attended by very senior officials from the Central Committee (from the Department of Cinematography).

At the time of the meeting neither Romm nor any of the others yet knew that Zhores had already been released. Each person had in front of him a copy of the telegram which Romm had sent to the Kaluga hospital at the very beginning of June. There was an accompanying letter with it, evidently from the Kaluga Party Committee and a certificate from the hospital which stated that Zhores was 'mentally ill and a public danger' and must be isolated from normal people. These documents had been written before 12 June.[1] Romm was taken to task for interfering in the affairs of the hospital and for insulting the Head Doctor of the hospital, Lifshits, whom Romm had accused of violating the Hippocratic oath. Furthermore, they said that Romm's telegram had been published abroad and broadcast on the BBC. This was a deliberate lie. The foreign press had only reported that Romm was among those protesting against the illegal committal of my brother, but neither his telegram nor any of the others had been broadcast by any foreign radio station or published in the papers. Naturally Romm denied all these unjust accusations. He said that he had composed his telegram at the Central Telegraph Office and hadn't even kept a copy. If the BBC had broadcast the text of this telegram, then it must have 'agents' at the Moscow telegraph office or at the Kaluga mental hospital.

[1] That is before the meeting with Academicians at the Ministry of Health.

Romm went on to say that he had seen Zhores very recently and found him to be completely sane. The meeting lasted two hours and at the end Romm said: 'If I find out that Zhores Medvedev was really ill and that the Kaluga hospital really helped him, then I will apologise to Lifshits. But if it turns out that there is nothing wrong with Zhores Medvedev and that the Kaluga hospital acted improperly, then we shall all assemble here again and you will apologise to me.'

On the same day Kaverin was called to a similar meeting at the Union of Writers, but this was at three o'clock in the afternoon. Several Secretaries and other high functionaries of the Union of Writers were there as well as a man Kaverin had never seen before. They had in front of them copies of Kaverin's telegrams to the Kaluga hospital and also a letter from Lifshits in which he justified the action of the hospital, explaining that Zhores Medvedev is 'mentally ill and a public danger'. This letter was written also before 12 June. There was a list of other writers who had written protests on the table—no doubt their sessions had been designated for different days. The assembled Secretaries began to attack Kaverin for his interference in the Medvedev affair and while they were at it, reproached him for previous 'sins' (including the famous letter of Kaverin to Fedin about Solzhenitsyn). Then all six members of this 'commission', not one of whom had even set eyes on Zhores, tried to convince Kaverin who had known my brother for about ten years, that Medvedev was in actual fact unbalanced. Kaverin, however, already knew that Zhores had been discharged from the hospital. After listening to all the accusations and eloquently dismissing them, Kaverin placed his copy of Lifshits's letter on the table in front of him and said, 'Actually the doctor contradicts himself. He writes in his letter that Zhores Medvedev is a public danger and mentally ill. Yet this same Lifshits today freed his dangerous patient and discharged him from the hospital. Right now Zhores is at home with his family.'

'What do you mean: *freed*?' one of the members of the commission exclaimed, and even jumped up from his chair. Kaverin explained and the meeting was adjourned, never to be reconvened.

On the same day Tvardovsky was also called by his Party Committee. The formal pretext was to introduce him to the Secretary of the Party Committee of his district (to which he had been transferred after leaving his post as editor of *Novy Mir*). However, five minutes after they had begun to talk, the Deputy Head of the Department of Culture of the Central Committee, A. Belyaev, came into the office. He began to criticise Tvardovsky for interfering in the case of the 'unbalanced' Zhores Medvedev. 'You know, we were going to give you a very different award,' he said to Tvardovsky without a trace of embarrassment.[1] (What kind of other decoration had been prepared for him by the Cultural Department of the Central Committee was not revealed.)

I also heard that in the middle of June several Party organisations had received instructions to start a special file on those Party members who had actively protested against Zhores's committal.

[1] Tvardovsky was given the Order of the Red Banner of Labour on his sixtieth birthday; this is a relatively minor award.

This badly timed spate of reprimands, though brought to a halt the next day, was nevertheless very revealing. It showed that the illegal hospitalisation of my brother was not just an isolated and accidental action in which only the local Kaluga authorities were involved. Neither the Minister of Health, Petrovsky (who had called in the Academicians on 12 June for a dressing-down), nor the officials of the Union of Writers or the Union of Cinematographers, let alone those more authoritative officials of the Central Committee, would have begun such an intensive campaign to defend the actions of the Kaluga mental hospital if the Kaluga Party Committee's appeal to them had not been backed up by extremely authoritative instructions from some *very* high quarter in Moscow. All this confirmed my guess that the strings of the affair were being manipulated from Moscow. However, we have not been able to find out who exactly was responsible and on what level the whole 'operation' had been planned.

On the morning of 18 June while I was waiting for my brother someone rang me from the KGB and asked me to come and see them at 3 pm. On arrival there, I was taken to one of the offices where I was immediately joined by a KGB official, evidently a very high-ranking one. His tone was friendly throughout, and he talked exclusively about my brother's case. He assured me that it had all been the work of the Kaluga health authorities and that the KGB, contrary to certain reports in the foreign press, had been in no way involved. I replied that I had indeed proceeded from the assumption that at the very highest level the KGB had played no part in mounting the 'operation' and had clearly been presented with a *fait accompli*. However, it was nevertheless obvious, I went on, that at a lower level (particularly as represented by its Kaluga branch), the KGB had been very active throughout the affair.

What they wanted to do now was to 'close the case'. I agreed, but only under certain conditions; above all, that the Kaluga hospital destroy the false medical record, that my brother should not be registered as an outpatient and that no file should be kept requiring him to appear at regular intervals for a check-up by psychiatrists. In other words, there must be absolutely no question of any further psychiatric blackmail, and my brother must be enabled to live and work like any normal person, without having to fear a possible repetition of committal at any time, simply if somebody happened to find it desirable. 'I shall regard any diagnosis of mental illness in my brother as a threat to myself as well—my brother and I are twins and we have an identical heredity.' However the KGB official promised nothing; he merely replied that my allegations about the involvement of local KGB organs in the affair would have to be carefully checked.

As I found out later, they did not keep their side of the bargain, which is the main reason for the writing of this account.

On the same day, 18 June, Sakharov was invited to the Central Committee to see the head of the Department of Science, Schools and Institutes of Higher Education, S. P. Trapeznikov. The conversation was lengthy and touched on many questions, but the main emphasis was on a letter to the Central Committee about the development of socialist democratisation, which had been sent in March 1970 and had been signed not only by Sakharov but also by Turchin and me. Sakharov, however, at the very beginning of the talk, raised Zhores's case. Trapeznikov answered that the Central Committee had nothing to do with the matter—those responsible were the local health authorities. He insisted that the Central Committee heard about the hospitalisation of Medvedev only after the fact and had to some extent helped to resolve the problem. He added, however, that Medvedev really seemed to some extent abnormal in his behaviour, even though the Kaluga doctors had gone too far.

It was already evening when I returned home and was able to talk properly with my brother for the first time in three weeks.

In the next few days I was busy at work and with preparations for a holiday. I very much needed to have a rest—as did Zhores—after all we had been through. On 23 June I left for the South and returned to Moscow only in August.

8

Freedom Without Freedom
17 June–1 September

ZHORES MEDVEDEV

WE got home from Kaluga at about two o'clock. Only when I was at last in my own apartment did I feel that the whole fantastic episode was over. My brother rang from Moscow and congratulated me on the happy conclusion to my psychiatric adventure. After dealing with various pressing matters and looking at my mail, I decided to listen to the radio. The freedom to choose whatever programme I wished was an enormous pleasure after uninterrupted exposure to the hospital loudspeaker which blared in the corridor from seven in the morning until ten in the evening. At about 5.50 I happened to tune in to the BBC. Suddenly I heard the announcer say that according to reports from foreign correspondents in Moscow, 'the biologist Zhores Medvedev has been freed from the Kaluga psychiatric hospital in which he had been confined after his arrest on 29 May . . .' After the news, the BBC commentator Maurice Latey gave a special talk on this event. His view was that my speedy release, so unexpected, was the result of a struggle between the scientists and the bureaucratic leadership, from which the scientists had emerged victorious. Latey went on to say that on 15 June there had been a special protest by Solzhenitsyn about the practice of putting absolutely sane dissident intellectuals into madhouses. The efficiency of the correspondents was astonishing, but as I learned later, information about my discharge had been given to them by semi-official sources.

On the evening of 17 June someone from Moscow brought me the text of Solzhenitsyn's statement and copies of many of the letters sent by scientists and writers to the various medical and other authorities concerned.

On 18 June, on arriving in Moscow, I was astonished to hear that the day before, when I was already free, two of my friends, the director Mikhail Romm and the writer Venyamin Kaverin, had been seriously criticised at a rather high level for sending protest telegrams.

These rather belated attempts to 'discipline' them could only be explained by some lack of co-ordination between those responsible for putting the psychiatric 'scenario' into effect and its creators. The medical officials involved could react to letters and telegrams of protest only in two ways: they could either ignore them, on the grounds that they were sent by persons incompetent to judge; or they could take account of them as coming from people familiar from many years' personal acquaintance with the man whose mental soundness they had been instructed to examine and call in question. But neither the Kaluga doctors nor even the Minister of Health had the authority to oblige the Committee on Cinematography or the

Secretariat of the Union of Writers to set up that kind of disciplinary meeting for eminent members of the Moscow intelligentsia. (Afterwards I found out that several other friends had also been called in on 16 and 17 June—by their district Party Committee, or the primary Party organisation at their place of work, or by the authorities of their institutes—and asked to explain their protests.) Instructions to call these meetings, together with copies of the relevant letters and telegrams, could only have come from some central body which would have been anything but a medical one. This central body must have been in touch with the Kaluga Party Committee or the local branch of the KGB in order to get the necessary documents. The psychiatric hospital did not have the right to make copies of letters and telegrams and send them to non-medical institutions. They should have filed all such materials in the medical case-history together with the information that Lifshits had gained in interviews with my colleagues and the administrative personnel at the Obninsk Institute of Radiology. Hospitals are supposed to keep all information about patients from whatever source strictly confidential, and it can be made available only to medical personnel. Handing over this kind of material to non-medical organisations such as the Committee on Cinematography or the Secretariat of the Union of Writers, and also to the Kaluga Party Committee, was a gross violation of medical ethics and of the Hippocratic oath (which in a modified form is also binding on Soviet doctors). This oath prohibits the divulging of information received by a doctor or its use to the detriment of the patient. Yet the disciplinary meetings of 16 and

17 June were undoubtedly a form of blackmail—directed at me as well as at those who had tried to help the doctors to arrive at an accurate understanding of the person they were dealing with and thus to make a proper diagnosis. These meetings, moreover, violated the general procedure for examining submissions made to a state organisation by private citizens. After 17 June there were no more such meetings.

On 18 June my brother was called to the central headquarters of the KGB and assured that they had no direct involvement in what had happened at Kaluga and Obninsk, and that the whole episode was the work of local authorities. They asked him not to write anything about what had happened, and to consider the case closed. My brother agreed on behalf of us both, but only if certain conditions were observed. What he insisted on was quite simply that there must be *mutual* action to wind up the whole business.

I had said something very similar to Lifshits during our final conversation at the hospital. When he asked me not to write up my hospital experience I replied that I didn't have the slightest inclination to do so. 'All the more,' I said, 'in that Anton Chekhov long ago described a case of a sane man being held in a mental hospital against his will, so the subject isn't exactly original.'

'Of course,' said Lifshits brightly, 'his famous story *Ward Number Six*.' With this observation our Kaluga doctor demonstrated a certain erudition in literary matters. But he must have forgotten that in the Chekhov story, the man who is lured by a trick to the ward for mental patients, after a secret but inconclusive examination, and is then beaten up during an attempt to escape, was none other than the Head Doctor of the provincial hospital in question. He soon died of an apoplectic stroke. Lifshifts had also overlooked the possibility that Chekhov himself might also have been forcibly hospitalised if the Lifshits criteria had been applied to him. By profession Chekhov was a doctor, and a very good one. His literary activity began as a pastime. He also wrote on politics and sociology; one need only recall his account of the life of the prisoners on Sakhalin.

'But I will not write about my time here,' I assured Lifshits, 'as long as you do not remind me of your existence by ever summoning me for any further examinations. If you try to keep up any form of psychiatric pressure, then I shall consider myself entirely free to protect myself as best I can.'

In the first days following my return home I learned about the widespread reaction to my illegal hospitalisation. Thanks to the many protests by scientists both in the USSR and abroad, the use of psychiatry as a means of persecution had attracted the attention of foreign commentators and journalists. Newspapers and weeklies in England, the United States, France and other countries not only published the numerous protests about this violation of medical ethics in the USSR, but also described the actual events in Obninsk and Kaluga. Colleagues and friends in different countries sent me clippings from newspapers and magazines. The bulk of these press cuttings, though usually sent by registered post, never reached me, but I received some of the materials all the same. They showed what strong feelings had been aroused. These are some of the headlines and titles of articles: 'Madhouse for opponents' (*The Times*), 'The dangers of speaking out' (*Nature*), 'A scientist in asylum' (*Reuters*), 'Protests by scientists in Soviet on biologist's arrest reported' (*New York Times*), 'Soviet scientists try to free their colleague' (*Daily Telegraph*). The *New York Times* alone had eight articles on the subject and several pieces were published in *Le Monde* and other papers. Judging by the foreign press, the whole thing developed into such a scandal that the decision to drop it was scarcely surprising. As a result of all this sensation, people became very curious about my manuscript on international scientific co-operation— and the foreign correspondents in Moscow tried very hard to get hold of it. By 6 or 7 June they somehow succeeded in getting a photocopy of excerpts from it and on 8 June several papers (the *Herald Tribune*, *Washington Post* and others) carried a story by the Moscow correspondent Anthony Astrachan: 'Soviet policy toward foreign travel criticised in Medvedev's book.' Astrachan wrote that excerpts from the book had become available to foreign correspondents on 7 June. He gave a summary of several sections with quotations that showed he really had seen an authentic text. Similar material appeared in the *New York Times* of 14 June and there were reports about the book in the English, German, French and Swedish press. I never found out who gave it to the correspondents. But they evidently didn't have the complete text because in their articles they only wrote about the first part, which happens to be the least important.

The leakage of information about this book was extremely unfortunate, because I did not regard it as a completed work, but it was now out of my control. In order to put the whole affair on an official basis, I sent a copy of the manuscript to the Moscow publishing house, 'International Relations', with an explanatory letter and a request that they consider the possibility of publishing it in some form in the USSR.

The *New York Times* and several other foreign papers also printed very distorted accounts of my other sociological work (this too was unfinished) on the problem of corresponding and exchanging information with persons abroad.[1] But references to this work were clearly based on rumours, and the text certainly had never become available to foreign correspondents. I immediately asked Professor Lerner and other foreign friends to take whatever measures necessary to prevent the 'pirated' publication of excerpts from these works in newspapers and other mass media. I heard that my friends successfully stopped *Time* magazine from publishing a chapter.

Two days after my return home, I began intensive efforts to get a job. During my final conversation with Lifshits he told me that the Institute of Medical Radiology had been instructed to reinstate me. His words seemed plausible in the light of an official visit I had received two days before my discharge from the hospital, when three members of the Institute's trade union committee brought me oranges and chocolates, purchased out of the committee's 'sick fund'. Such consideration for a colleague, dismissed more than a year before, could well be interpreted as a 'good-will mission' and would have been impossible without the

[1] *Secrecy of Correspondence is Guaranteed by Law.*

approval of the Institute's directors. But when I began to make inquiries in Obninsk and at the Academy of Medical Sciences about my reinstatement, it seemed that the benevolent interest shown in my fate which had prompted the visit of the three trade union officials was exceedingly short-lived. When I went to see Comrade Ponomar, the head of the Personnel Department of the AMS, to make official arrangements for my appointment as a senior research assistant, and later when I talked to the Secretary of the AMS, Snezhnevsky, they both informed me that my reinstatement to a post in Obninsk had run up against various difficulties, and that the problem of finding me a position would be dealt with by the Academy of Sciences. The President of the Academy of Sciences, Keldysh, had officially promised at the meeting on 12 June at the Ministry of Health to find me a post in one of the institutes of the Academy, and had said that there already was such a post waiting for me in the Academy's biological centre at Pushchino. I went immediately to the Academy and left a written request, addressed to Keldysh, formally applying for this post in Pushchino and also asking him to grant me a personal interview. In a few days I was called in by the head of the personnel department of the Academy of Sciences, Comrade Tsipkin, and informed that Keldysh had considered my request and had come to an understanding with the science department of the Central Committee and the Kaluga Party Committee that I would after all be reinstated at the Institute of Medical Radiology:

'He [Keldysh] asked me to tell you to wait for a week or ten days, in the course of which you will be

approached with an offer of work. He also asked me
to tell you that you must not make difficulties—please
agree to whatever they su ;gest.'

I waited ten days, but nobody got in touch with
me. In Keldysh's office they were quite astonished and
promised to report it to him. I decided in any case to
take the initiative myself and went to see the director
of the Institute of Medical Radiology, G. A. Zed-
genidze. But he categorically rejected any possibility
of my reinstatement there. After ten more days had
passed I was told by the personnel department of the
Academy of Sciences that the question of finding me
a position had been settled and that in a very few days
I would be made an offer. This time Tsipkin was
speaking the truth. At the beginning of August I was
visited at home without any phone call beforehand by
representatives from the Institute of the Biochemistry
and Physiology of Agricultural Animals (in Borovsk,
near Kaluga) and offered a post in that Institute on the
biochemistry of ageing. I agreed at once and two days
later went to Borovsk to see the director. He was
most cordial and from the way he talked it looked as
though they had only been waiting for me to lose my
job in Obninsk in order to offer me a position at their
Institute. We agreed about the details, and the director
said that in two or three days he would ring me to
finalise everything. I waited for more than a week but
I never heard from him and then went to Borovsk to
find out what had happened. It turned out that the
Institute was under the jurisdiction of the Lenin
Agricultural Academy, where there had been certain
opposition to my appointment.

I went back to the AMS and to the Ministry of

Health with further requests for help in getting work, but in both places they refused to do anything, telling me that only the President of the Academy of Sciences could deal with my problem. I was back where I had started.

But even before these difficulties arose about Borovsk, there was a small incident which in fact prompted me to write the present account.

At the end of June I was telephoned by a nurse from the Obninsk Psychiatric Clinic. In a calm matter-of-fact voice, as if it were self-evident, she asked me to come to the outpatient department for a routine check-up. At first I thought that they were again interested in my son and had got the names wrong, so I asked her to tell me who exactly she wanted and what for. But there was no mistake.

'You have just been treated in the Kaluga hospital,' said the nurse, 'and now they have sent us your papers and you are registered with us in the outpatient department. Under the rules we have to keep a regular check on the patient's condition for our records.'

Of course, I told her what she could do with her records, and demanded that they stop this psychiatric blackmail. But my wife rushed off to the clinic. According to the regulations, the family must be told the diagnosis and the symptoms of illness, but neither Lifshits nor Bondareva had done this. In the Obninsk outpatient department they also didn't want to tell my wife anything at first, but she was so insistent that at last they showed her the card they had received for their file—since it had been written up in Kaluga the Obninsk clinic could not be held responsible for it. Bondareva had signed it and quoted the findings of the 'commission' of psychiatrists (listing the names and positions of the two Morozovs, Nadzharov and Lifshits) and formulated the diagnosis of the 'illness' as follows: 'incipient schizophrenia' accompanied by 'paranoid delusions of reforming society'. The basic symptoms of the 'illness' were also described on the card: 'split personality, expressed in the need to combine scientific work in his field with publicist activities; an overestimation of his own personality, a deterioration in recent years of the quality of his scientific work, an exaggerated attention to detail in his publicist writing, lack of a sense of reality, poor adaptation to the social environment'. The hospital recommended 'outpatient treatment and employment'.

In August I received a letter from the United States from my friend, Professor Leonard Hayflick, head of the Department of Medical Microbiology at Stanford University. After congratulating me on my release, Hayflick continued:

> As you may know, when we learned about what happened to you I wrote a series of personal letters to many of my friends in the Soviet Union asking them to do all they could in order to help you. I received only two replies, and am enclosing photocopies of them in this letter . . .[1]

The two letters were from Academician V. A. Engelhardt, Director of the Institute of Molecular Biology of the Academy of Sciences, and V. I. Khozinsky, head of a laboratory at the Institute of Poliomyelitis and

[1] This is a translation back into English from Russian.

Virus Encephalitis of the AMS. Academician Engelhardt has known me personally for a very long time,
but I have never ever met Khozinsky. Both letters
were official, on institute stationery; Engelhardt wrote
in English, Khozinsky in Russian. Since these letters
were sent abroad without being marked confidential,
I feel free to quote them here in full:

> Dear Professor Hayflick,
> I received your letter of 22 June with some delay
> after returning from a long trip.
> As you obviously must know from reports in
> the press, Dr Zhores Medvedev was discharged
> from the hospital on 17 June. During my brief stay
> in Moscow between two trips, we had a short talk
> and I was glad to find him sane and safe. He was in
> good form and is okay—the anxiety over this un-
> happy episode is over.
> Yours sincerely,
> Professor V. A. Engelhardt[1]

The letter from Khozinsky was rather different:

> Dear Professor Hayflick,
> I have made inquiries and found out that Dr
> Zhores Medvedev was treated for a short time in
> the Kaluga Psychiatric Hospital in connection with
> the aggravation of an incipient schizophrenic con-
> dition. At present he continues to be treated at home.
> The question of his future employment will be
> decided after he is again completely well. There has
> been no threat to his physical safety nor will there
> be.

[1] This is also a translation back into English from Russian.

I regret that you have been a victim of unverified rumours and can assure you that scientific freedom and democracy in the Soviet Union are protected by the Constitution and nobody has the right to violate it.

I am sure that you are profoundly concerned not only about the fate of scientists but also about the physical safety of the many hundreds of thousands of simple people in Vietnam, Cambodia and the Middle East. If you find it possible to add your voice to those who are demanding an end to mass murder in these parts of the world, then you may be sure that my colleagues and I will regard any such step of yours with the greatest sympathy and support.

Sincerely yours,

V. I. Khozinsky, Doctor of Biology

Head of Laboratory at the Institute of Poliomyelitis and Virus Encephalitis of the AMN of the USSR

It goes without saying that Khozinsky and those who supplied him with these official medical details were violating elementary medical ethics which strictly forbid the divulgence of information about the diagnosis and history of a patient's illness. The Kaluga hospital and the organisers of the affair, even after my discharge, felt free to disregard all the usual rules and to spread 'psychiatric' information about me not only in the Soviet Union but also abroad. Khozinsky may well have believed what he wrote in his letter, but there can be no doubt whatsoever of his utter dishonesty and lack of decency. Where did he get his story about my 'treatment being continued at home' and work being found for me only after I am completely well? He should know that one never completely recovers from schizophrenia, there are only remissions.

There may have been similar demagogic replies to other letters from foreign scientists. And the only way to put a stop to all this once and for all is to write a complete account of what actually happened with all the necessary 'attention to detail'.

It was now plain that in spite of the discharge, they were still declaring me mad and branding my work on the history and sociology of science as 'reformist delusion'. But in any case, at last I knew the diagnosis. I borrowed a psychiatry textbook for medical students from one of my friends, the latest edition of *Psychiatry*, written by O. V. Kerbikov, M. V. Korkina, R. A. Nadzharov and A. V. Snezhnevsky, and published in 1968. I began to study my own 'illness' with great fascination. Schizophrenia, according to the textbook, has many forms, but all of them have certain features in common. Characteristic of all form is:

the disintegration of the psyche and a resulting lack of co-ordination between its activity and external stimuli that becomes apparent in the patient's behaviour. His behaviour no longer corresponds to the conditions of his life and surroundings, becoming erratic and incomprehensible. For example, a man who is an accountant by profession and has never shown the least interest in biology or medicine, suddenly goes to a meeting of biologists and tries to address them on the origins of organic matter. Or a ticket collector on a train starts asking passengers not only for their tickets, but also for their marriage certificate . . . Such oddities of behaviour are accompanied by a growing lack of interest in any kind of activity and a loss of normal desires. Such persons for no apparent reason give up their work, abandon their studies, stop seeing their friends and relatives, and spend whole days in bed, neglecting their personal appearance. The disintegration of the psyche, its derangement, clearly affects the thought processes and consequently the person's speech and writing. His grammar may be relatively intact, but there are no logical connections or sense. There are subject and predicate and subordinate clauses, but it is difficult or impossible to grasp the meaning of what he says or writes. One woman patient, for example, wrote to her doctor:

'To rely on your circumspection which is doubtless conducted more substantially than your respectability for unforeseen circumstances in any convention falls to the lot of my faithful rules in the execution of which I find myself in indisputability state beforehand by you.'

Further on the textbook lists other features common to all forms of schizophrenia: 'emotional disturbances, apathy, loss of feeling, emotional insensitivity, hallucinations, automatism, etc.' The paranoid form which the doctors had 'diagnosed' in me, according to the textbook

is characterised by the prevalence of delusions, often accompanied by hallucination. Delusions can take on many different forms: delusions of having certain connections of influence, delusions of jealousy and persecution, delusions involving invention or litigation, hypochondria or megalomania. Although the actual development of a paranoid state varies from case to case, one may note that as a general rule delusions have a tendency to stabilise for lengthy periods and form a systematic pattern which, however gradually, breaks down as the patient's intellectual capacity diminishes. As the disintegration of the psyche progresses, so the system of paranoid delusion also collapses.

But the authors of the textbook do not prognosticate an immediate 'disintegration of the psyche' in a case like mine because 'incipient schizophrenia' takes a long time before reaching the stage of 'apathetic imbecility'.

Despite his systematised pattern of delusions, the patient is able over a long period to fulfil his professional obligations. But at the same time his behaviour is often determined by the nature of his delusions which may lead him to dangerous aggression against imaginary persecutors and corresponding attempts to protect himself against them by appealing to different organisations, to public opinion, or by pestering others with demands to give effect to his delusional ideas and projects. The patient is proud, has a feeling of his own dignity, expresses himself dogmatically and is convinced of the supreme value and infallibility of his views.

In the opinion of the authors of the textbook, schizophrenia as a rule is incurable. Ultimately, after extended or brief periods of remission, the disintegration of the psyche takes place. The patient's speech becomes meaningless and incoherent, with the artificial stringing together of distorted words in combinations dominated by assonance and alliteration.

It is not a very cheerful prospect, a very terrible one in fact. No wonder that Alexander Pushkin, who was also 'ill-adapted' to the social environment of his time, was afraid of losing his mind. Perhaps it was the fate of Chaadaev which inspired his poem about this fear, or perhaps it was a contemporary textbook on psychiatry:

> God forbid that I should lose my mind,
> Easier by far the beggar's lot,
> Easier by far the labourer's hungry toil.
> Not that I so greatly prize
> My reason, or cannot bear the thought
> Of parting with it:
>
> If only I were left
> In freedom, how merrily
> I'd run to dark forest groves
> And sing in feverish hallucination
> Forgetting myself in a haze
> Of strange, disordered visions.
>
> I'd listen rapturously to the waves
> And gaze in blissful concentration
> At the empty heavens up above,
> And then I'd be as strong and free
> As a whirlwind raging in the fields,
> Uprooting forests in its path.

But here's the rub: if you go mad,
They'll fear you worse than any plague
And lock you up at once
Putting you on a chain—an idiot
Whom they'll come to mock
As they would a captured beast,
Through its prison bars.

And then at night I'd hear
Not the ringing song of nightingales
Or the whispering of trees,
But the frenzied cries of comrades,
The curses of my madhouse guards,
And on my limbs the grind of clanking irons.[1]

[1] Translated by Max Hayward.

9

Psycho-adaptation or Democratisation?

THE detailed examples given in the textbook of psychiatry of the symptoms of 'incipient schizophrenia' with 'paranoid delusions' give a clear picture of what they meant by a 'split personality'. My case was hardly a very typical one, since my publicist and sociological works had, after all, something to do with genetics, gerontology and the exchange of scientific information. They were thus not all that remote from my basic professional interests. But we do not have far to seek for much more graphic illustrations than those quoted in the textbook, such as the accountant with his sudden interest in the origins of life, or the ticket collector asking people for their marriage certificates. Take, for example, that outstanding figure whom we all remember so well as an economist, a military leader, philosopher, statesman and diplomat. And suddenly out of the blue he publishes his article on the problems of linguistics and personally begins to introduce tangerine and eucalyptus trees to the Crimea. Then there was that other great leader, also wise politician, diplomat, economist, agricultural specialist and historian of the Party. Suddenly he begins to make decisions about the architecture of apartment houses, arbitrates in a disagreement between two different schools of genetics, disbands ministries, creates regional economic councils, divides Party committees into agricultural and industrial sections, tries to grow maize in the North, forbids the private ownership of cattle in the countryside and teaches writers the secrets of their craft. And of each of them it was true to say that they were proud, expressed themselves dogmatically and were convinced of the supreme value and infallibility of their views. Of course eucalyptus trees never got accustomed to the Crimea and maize doesn't grow in the North, but the behaviour of both of these men continued to be determined by the nature of their delusions without adapting to reality. The behaviour of one of them was further aggravated by persecution mania and sadism—which led him to spend a lot of time 'discovering' imaginary conspiracies, introducing draconian laws, organising mass arrests, executions and tortures, and he was completely isolated in a world of his own. But these were particularly bad cases. Milder and less dangerous forms of the same condition are extremely common and evoke little surprise. One comes across them in almost every biography. My son, for example, is reading a book about V. I. Dahl called *A Man Collects Words* published in 1969. Dahl was a surgeon by training—he graduated from the Faculty of Medicine at the same time as the famous Pirogov. He was Head of Chancellery at the Ministry of Internal Affairs. But besides this, he was a philologist and a collector of words who compiled the famous *Explanatory Dictionary of the Russian Language*. Under a pseudonym he wrote stories and political articles. At last, of course, it was understood that this was a split personality (in fact it seemed to be split in three). On the personal order of the Tsar, Dahl was called in by his Minister who said to him: 'You must choose, my dear sir—either be a writer and do not serve—or serve, and do not write.'

I have in front of me another book, *They Hid their Names* (on the history of pseudonymous and anonymous writing), by V. G. Dmitriev. He gives hundreds of classical examples of split personalities. The author of *Alice in Wonderland*, Lewis Carroll, in fact was the mathematician Charles Dodgson. That strange author who published seven volumes of children's fairy tales, novels and stories under the pen-name 'Puss-in-Boots' was in real life a professor of zoology, N. P. Vagner.

But many examples come to mind without the help of books. The leading British biochemist and geneticist J. B. S. Haldane wrote detective novels under a pseudonym, and then all of a sudden became an editor of the Communist *Daily Worker* and devoted his time to sociology and journalism. Gregor Mendel, a priest and Father Superior of a monastery, suddenly got fascinated by biology and used his free time to cross-breed peas and discover the laws of heredity. Spinoza, who had been highly successful at his profession of polishing lenses, all at once felt drawn to philosophy. Andrei Gromyko, a graduate of the Minsk Livestock Institute, later went into diplomacy and became Minister of Foreign Affairs. The brilliant chemist Linus Pauling, who received the Nobel Prize for chemistry, took up political activity with such success that he was awarded both the Nobel and Lenin Peace Prizes. There are a great number of 'split personalities' among my immediate friends and acquaintances: the geneticist Raissa Berg holds exhibitions of her own abstract paintings and writes satirical novels; Sakharov, the physicist and mathematician, has written an interesting essay on the problems of intellectual freedom and peaceful eo-existence; the biophysicist B. V. Volkenshtein writes publicist works and critical essays on literature; the agricultural chemist V. M. Klechkovsky suddenly began to interest himself in complex problems of mathematical physics. One could go on quoting examples like this for ever. Any hobby becomes a psychiatric danger. And if one goes back further in time, there were Aristotle, Leonardo da Vinci, Lomonosov and others whose minds went off in so many directions that it was in most cases not split personality, but complete fragmentation of the intellect. Happily there was no psychiatry in those days, and madmen were judged simply on the basis of common sense and sometimes even revered, as, for example, Vassily the Blessed in Moscow.[1]

The second symptom recorded on my card as a sign of schizophrenia was my 'exaggerated opinion' of myself or 'overestimation' of my own personality—this was even harder to pin down. I owed it no doubt to my description of myself as a 'scientist of average capability'. Since I had been dismissed from my post, it followed that I should have put myself in a lower category, because scientists of average capability usually keep their jobs. On the other hand, if I had shown too much modesty, then the psychiatrists

[1] The 'simple-minded' saint after whom the church in Red Square is named.

could have written in their diagnosis that I had an
'inadequate opinion of myself' or 'underestimated'
my own personality—and in the eyes of psychiatry
it would have been much the same. In mental hospitals,
one patient calls himself Napoleon or Socrates while
another suffers from a sense of his own worthlessness,
or is convinced that he has contracted leprosy or
syphilis.

Recalling my conversations with Lifshits, I decided
that the only symptom which the psychiatrists
seriously tried to find grounds for was the third one,
namely 'a deterioration of the quality of his scientific
work in recent years'. My wife came to the same
conclusion. It was clear from conversations we both
had with him that Lifshits had obtained a list of my
scientific publications of various years from the
personnel department of the Institute of Medical
Radiology and had actually read some of them.
These conversations with Lifshits struck me as being
the most fantastic of all. By collecting some sort of
evidence of my intellectual decline, he hoped somehow
to disguise his fake diagnosis. Neither G. Morozov
or Lunts would have bothered to study one of their
patients so thoroughly. Lifshits said that he had read
two of my books on biochemistry and felt that the
second book, published by the State Medical Publishing House in 1968, was much inferior to the first,
published in 1963. Above all he was unhappy about
the fact that the second book on the molecular-genetic
mechanism in the development of an organism was
more theoretical than the first which dealt with the
biosynthesis of albumen. He tried to convince both
me and my wife that my experimental work carried

out before 1962 in the Timiryazev Academy was much
better than all the work done afterwards at the Institute of Medical Radiology. G. Morozov advanced
the same argument in support of the 'diagnosis'
during the meeting at the Ministry of Health, but the
Academicians laughed him out of court, observing
that the quality of a piece of work in biochemistry
can only be judged by specialists—by biochemists—
and not by psychiatrists. Apart from this, however,
everyone knows that all scientists have a so-called
'age-curve' relating to the quality and quantity of
work they are able to do, the dynamics of scientific
productivity is now a subject of special research. There
are many factors here, but the chief one is simply that
of the decrease of the number of nerve cells and the
fact that they cannot replace themselves. Between
the ages of twenty and sixty, nerve cells decrease by
approximately fifty per cent in all people, and the
result is a matter of everybody's experience—the
progressive weakening of memory, for example. The
period of maximum productivity for physicists and
mathematicians, according to the book *Science about
Science* (Kiev, 1966), is between twenty and thirty,
for biologists between thirty and forty. Since I had
become forty-five in 1970, I was already past my
prime. But this is totally irrelevant to a diagnosis of
schizophrenia.

This obviously leaves as the main grounds for the
diagnosis, the symptom described as 'poor adaptation
to the social environment', and it was the one which
led to the conclusion about my being a public danger.
But in this respect the Kaluga doctors and the Moscow
specialists were taking a much broader view of the

problem than was warranted by their science. They were encroaching on another field here, borrowing the all too familiar 'class approach' to the concept of social adaptation. In our discussions, both Lifshits and Bondareva recognised that in the ordinary everyday sense I was normally adapted to the environment. They had forcibly committed to the hospital as a 'public danger' someone who had never been tried in court—even in a civil case—never been picked up by the police for a breach of the peace, and never once been fined for anything, had never been divorced, did not smoke or drink, had never been reprimanded at work and never had violent quarrels with anyone. On the other hand, their 'patient' always took his place in the parades on state holidays, attended seminars, subscribed to newspapers and journals, was a member of the society Znanie (Knowledge), was the chairman of a Comrades' Court, went to the theatre and cinema, had friends, loved to dig in the garden, ride a bicycle, go canoeing, read *Novy Mir* and American detective stories and listen to light music. In general I led the quiet existence of a provincial scientist—nothing could have been more average and normal or less exotic. Medical investigation of my personality could go no further than this—nor should it, because by looking into my views and outlook, my attitude towards policies, it meant leaving medicine for politics. Lifshits did in fact cross this boundary line, though very reluctantly. Having been ordered to check on the psychological condition of an Obninsk scientist, he had at first hoped to find something that really was within his professional competence, something strange in my behaviour or scientific output, something incomprehensible to others, something outlandish, such as megalomania or a persecution complex, a striving to dominate or impose my views, attempts to devise fantastic and unreal projects. He was very anxious not to reduce it to a question of political motives. This is why he studied my scientific publications and collected rumours and gossip about me, hoping to find some grounds or other for quieting his professional conscience. At the Serbsky Institute in Moscow, they evidently take a much simpler and more cynical view, but for a provincial doctor it was all very complicated. To make matters worse, there was constant pressure on him from all sides to get results. But he obviously couldn't find anything to indicate schizophrenia or mania—the only possible grounds for compulsory hospitalisation. And so Lifshits had decided to avoid seizing me at home or in the street and altered the scenario so that I myself would come to the psychiatric hospital, or at least to the clinic. But this didn't work. It was then that he had turned to the police for help. This was why he subsequently had to search for more serious diagnostic grounds to justify keeping me in hospital for 'treatment'. Finally he was ordered to do just this, but it required the involvement of a group of Moscow psychiatrists in the business of fabricating the evidence. At the beginning, however, their diagnosis was too mild. In August I learned that the Moscow commission had found only 'paranoid tendencies with reformist delusions', with no indication whatsoever of schizophrenia. This did not amount to very much, and some members of the commission even believed they had shown courage limiting themselves to such a minor falsification. The fact is that 'paranoid tendencies' and 'paranoia' are two entirely different things. The term 'paranoid tendencies' says nothing about the stage of the illness, which could still be only just beginning and imperceptible to others. 'Paranoia', on the other hand, is the fully fledged form of the disease, and like schizophrenia, is also a pathological process. This would have been a more serious and hopeless diagnosis. All the authorities needed from the doctors both in Kaluga and Moscow was a diagnosis of 'reformist delusions', and they didn't care how it was dressed up—whether it was called 'schizophrenia', 'paranoia' or 'paranoid tendencies' was a matter for the professionals. The Moscow specialists wanted the diagnosis to be as mild as possible—they, after all, were not answerable for the use of force. But the Kaluga doctors needed some more serious justification, and so they had to spice 'reformist tendencies' with the idea that I was a danger to the public or to myself. They must also have succeeded in convincing the Moscow doctors that another garnish was needed for my 'reformist delusions', but it could be that Bondareva added to her sins by falsely quoting their authority on this. 'Reformist delusion' is encountered in relatively mild types of mental illness and, according to the textbook on psychiatry, is not characterised by schizophrenic lack of logic but may to all intents and purposes be internally consistent. 'It may take the form,' to quote the textbook, 'of some fantastic or unreal project, for example, an elaborate plan to create an "Academy of universal happiness", or the discovery of a new principle for the classification of human knowledge, and is accompanied by a condition of the type known as "monomania".' People suffering from this kind of reformist delusion present no obvious danger to those around them or to themselves, and the regulations do not provide for them to be committed against their will to mental hospitals. A man who spends his time writing a great tome on the creation of a society where prosperity will be universal, where everyone will be happy and each receive according to his needs, cannot be a public danger *in the psychiatric sense*. Lunts, whom we have mentioned before as the leading authority in the field of 'special examination',[1] says in one of his recent works that a mentally ill person is a public danger if there is a chance that he may attack those around him, commit breaches of the peace, arson, robbery, murder or other such crimes. We know only too well, of course, that there have been maniacs and fanatics with 'reformist delusions' who have been capable of carrying out mass murder, terror, genocide —the list includes Nero, Hitler, Himmler, Yezhov, Beria, Stalin . . . But it is not only reformers who may be responsible for such acts of psychopathological violence against the masses. Conservatives may act in a similar fashion to preserve an existing order of injustice and privilege. However, those works of mine ascribed to 'reformist delusion' by Lifshits and Shostakovich (the others hadn't read them) could scarcely be termed a public danger in this sense. Even less were they definable as 'schizophrenic delusion' since this never has a logically consistent structure. I should remind both my readers and the actors in this sorry

[1] For the meaning of the term 'special examination', see above, page 100.

tale that one infallible test can be applied. It is true that works written in a state of schizophrenic delusion are sometimes published—at the author's own expense or even in the ordinary way. Indeed we all know cases of absolute gibberish being published in preference to works that are lucid and comprehensible. One of my Leningrad colleagues even collects books by schizophrenics—and already has about a hundred of them. The main point, however, is that this sort of thing can only be published in the original language— *any translation into a foreign language is quite impossible,* since neither the translator nor readers would be able to grasp the author's meaning. Therefore, when Lifshits after the invasion of my apartment on 29 May alleged that I had published my work on international co-operation abroad, he was *ipso facto* discounting the possibility of its being a product of schizophrenic delusion. The criterion of translation into other languages is certainly no guarantee of the scientific accuracy of a text or its truthfulness. As we know, numerous pseudo-scientific works are translated into other languages. But if we begin to put people into madhouses on the grounds that they have written books or articles in which something is untrue, or contradicts accepted dogma, or criticises, exposes or attacks the existing order of things—then the mind boggles at what might happen throughout the world. On winning the elections in England, the Conservatives would put all their Labour opponents into lunatic asylums, German Social Democrats would denounce Christian Democrats as schizophrenic and paranoiac, Catholics would demand compulsory hospitalisation for Protestants and Muslims would do the same to all infidels and atheists. The democratic French would fear the madhouse in totalitarian Spain, not to speak of Greece. The Warsaw Pact armies, having come to the assistance of Dubcek's opponents in Czechoslovakia, should have immediately proceeded to the building of mental hospitals to be staffed by imported psychiatrists. At the United Nations headquarters they would have to build a huge psychiatric clinic so that debates on controversial problems could take place under the supervision of international psychiatric commissions. The Glavlit censors would have to take courses in psychiatry and be given the right not only to prevent publication or make cuts in the text but also to dispatch authors for psychiatric examination. Articles submitted to scientific journals, apart from the usual security clearance, would also now require a doctor's certificate. Would such a world be normal? It is difficult to say, but it would appear that the first experiments in psycho-adaptation have already begun in this country.

Almost everywhere in the world the nature of society is such that there are least two professions, medicine and law, which are not part of the state system. This means that doctors and lawyers are concerned with the interests of their patients and clients and not with those of government authorities. Above all they are expected to observe the principle of professional secrecy. Totalitarian centralisation of the medical service, while introducing the progressive principle of free health care for all, has also made it possible to use medicine as a means of government control and political regulation. Medical 'dossiers' in clinics and hospitals are available to government officials, and a growing number of institutions and agencies ask for reports about a person's state of health with details of his past medical history and symptoms. Psychiatrists are playing an increasingly important role in all this—they may secretly veto a young person's entry to an academic institution, or a trip abroad—even only as a tourist—or pronounce on his suitability for many categories of employment. The medical record kept in a clinic or outpatient department may cause a man as much trouble as a court conviction or Jewish origin. As a result people are beginning to be afraid of psychiatric hospitals, resorting to them only in cases of extreme necessity. This puts doctors in a false position, impeding the early diagnosis of illness which could be cured or stabilised by modern drug treatment. In medicine, as in industry, centralisation makes impossible the sort of flexibility on which efficiency depends. It is a well known fact that in countries where patients are treated by private general practitioners as well as in specialised clinics, many illnesses are diagnosed at earlier stages. This has always been obvious in the case of 'embarrassing' diseases (such as those of the urinary tract, gynaecological and proctal diseases, etc.) and particularly cancer—people are simply afraid of cancer clinics and hospitals and finally turn to them when it is too late. Now the same is true for mental illness, although for entirely different reasons. The use of psychiatry to persecute dissidents only heightens people's fears and therefore reduces the availability of psychiatric help for those who really require it. If things go on like this, it will end with healthy, sane people sitting in madhouses while dangerous mental cases will walk about freely, denied the treatment they need.

This abuse of psychiatry is not, incidentally, new or original. It has been known for centuries already, although not on a mass scale. Under Alexander I, the cadet Zhukov was declared insane because he wrote a collection of verse about freedom. In his letter Alexander Solzhenitsyn mentions the fate of Chaadaev, the famous Russian philosopher, publicist and friend of Pushkin. Petr Yakovlevich Chaadaev, having returned to Russia after lengthy residence in several European countries, was astounded by the tyranny which prevailed under Nicholas I. One of his sharply critical 'Philosophical Letters' was published in French in the Moscow Journal *Telescope*. It was denounced to the Tsar by the Chief of the Secret Police, and Nicholas commented as follows: 'I consider this to be a farrago of insolent nonsense, worthy of a lunatic.' Thereupon the publisher of the journal, Nadezhdin, was exiled to Ust-Sysolsk and Chaadaev was publicly declared insane in a statement the original text of which has been preserved:

The essay of P. Y. Chaadaev which appeared in the *Telescope* and the thoughts expressed in it have aroused feelings of anger and repugnance in all Russians without exception. But the horror quickly turned to sympathy when they learned that their unhappy compatriot, the author of the article, suffers from derangement and insanity. Taking into consideration the unwell state of this unfortunate person, the Government in its solicitude and fatherly concern for its subjects, forbids him to leave his house and will provide free medical care with a special doctor to be appointed by the local authorities from among those under their jurisdiction.

Even then—at least in this case—the doctor was a government employee.

Chaadaev was put under psychiatric house arrest for about a year, and then having received the right to appear in society again, continued his literary and political activity.[1] However, he decided not to publish two other 'Philosophical Letters' in Russia, and during the author's lifetime they appeared only in France. The remaining 'Philosophical Letters' (there were eight in all) were published many years after his death.

A. S. Griboedov was also once denounced as a madman by high society. Rumours about it were so persistent that for a long time his friends continued to inquire about his health. Griboedov later used this episode in his verse drama *Woe From Wit* in which high society accuses Chatsky of being mad. Every schoolchild knows Famusov's speech explaining why intellectuals in the Russia of his day went out of their minds:

[1] (Footnote by Roy Medvedev.) The fate of Ekaterina Dmitrievna Panova, *née* Ulybysheva, to whom Chaadaev dedicated his 'Philosophical Letters' was even more tragic. At the request of her husband, this young woman was subjected to an examination with the object of determining the state of her mental faculties. In response to questions, she said that she was thirty-two years old, had been married for fifteen years and did not have any children. When they asked her whether she honoured the spiritual and civil laws, she replied: 'As to civil law, I am a republican—during the war with Poland I prayed for the Poles because they were fighting for freedom.' Panova was judged to be in a deranged mental state and put in a madhouse. Chaadaev wrote a letter to the Moscow Chief of Police stating that he had never discussed his 'Philosophical Letters' with Panova. We do not know what finally happened to her.

Learning—there's the plague,
The reason why the world has never
known so many lunatics, mad deeds,
mad words.

A citizen of Russia, M. Kologrivov, was put in a lunatic asylum by special decree of the Senate for his participation in the French Revolution of 1830. The decree read as follows: 'Whereas he did conduct himself as a madman, as a madman he shall be punished.' (The Senate had the right to determine 'mental fitness' since a decree of Peter the Great in 1721: 'On the Certification of Imbeciles by the Senate.' This 'certification' was something in the nature of a military examination for sons of the nobility who attempted to evade military service by pleading feeble-mindedness.)

But all these were isolated cases. Under Stalin, psychiatric reprisal became rather more widespread. However Stalin had more effective and speedy means of terror at his disposal. According to S. P. Pisarev[1] there were only a hundred persons in the psychiatric prison-hospitals in Kazan and Leningrad at the time of the mass rehabilitations (in 1956). They had usually ended up in these institutions after 'special examination' by the Serbsky Institute of Forensic Psychiatry, and were released in the same way as other people rehabilitated at this time.

---

[1] Former Party official who after diagnosis by the Serbsky Institute in 1953, was confined in psychiatric hospitals for almost two years—he had sent a report to Stalin on the misdeeds of the security organs. Released on the personal intervention of the Procurator-General, he sent a report to the Central Committee describing his experience in finding normal people, including eminent scholars and writers, confined indefinitely with the mentally ill.

The process of partial democratisation and restoration of legality which began after the Twentieth Congress apparently put an end to the political use of psychiatry for a time. But since this process did not go very deep and was soon brought to a halt, the authorities once more needed to find ways and means of punishing people for undesirable ideas and publications. Political trials of individual writers, poets and publicists (Brodsky, Sinyavsky, Daniel, Ginsburg, Galanskov and several others) showed, however, that normal legal processes with all they entail— the provision of evidence, defence lawyers, pretrial investigation to establish guilt, the judge's summing up of the legal aspects in court, the right of the accused to make a final plea, etc.—were a great embarrassment to the organisers of these trials and provoked indignation both in the Soviet Union and abroad. Such trials, in fact, only led to the further spread of 'sedition' and to a steady growth in the number of critical documents circulating in *samizdat*— a chain reaction of dissent.

Stalin's method was very simple. His rule was utterly arbitrary and lawless. After the exposure of some of Stalin's crimes, his successors affirmed the principle of strict legality, but they soon came up against numerous difficulties created by the contrast between the relatively democratic Constitution of the USSR and the by no means democratic system of government. It was frequently necessary to punish people who had not in fact gone beyond the bounds of what was permitted by law. 'Mild' repression such as dismissal from work was not always very effective. And then someone had the simple idea that the increasing number of political trials and political prisoners made a very poor public impression, while an increase in the number of patients under treatment in hospitals would be a very good indication of social progress. From this moment the psychiatric hospitals began to expand.

At present I know of many instances of people being put away in mental hospitals for political reasons—because they advocated certain social reforms or changes, for publishing works abroad or for expressing a determined wish to emigrate. I shall not describe these cases because I do not know the people concerned or the details of their stories. But I have read in *samizdat* manuscript form several works classified as the product of 'reformist delusions', and can say with absolute certainty that they are written by people in their right minds who are honest and patriotic advocates of the democratisation of our society in the interests of their country and the world at large. The same works were regarded rather differently by the psychiatrists, and I can quote some of the labels applied to them in the findings of 'special examinations': 'obsessive delusion of being a champion of truth and justice', 'over-concern with detail in his mental processes', 'inability to judge his situation', 'paranoid reformist delusions', 'pathological development of the personality with reformist delusions and incipient arterio-sclerosis of the brain', etc. Among the descriptions of symptoms of illness I have seen the following: 'He talked a great deal and heatedly argued his point of view, trying to impose it on others', 'was dictatorial', 'stands out by his behaviour, was an activist . . . gathered a crowd around him . . . shouted that he would fight for truth and democracy'.

Now, at the end of this account, I want to stress that it certainly has *not* been written because I feel that there is anything shameful about mental illness. Illness is not a vice, but a misfortune which calls for sympathy and compassion. For both patient and doctor, the struggle with mental illness may be arduous and heroic. Mental illness is widespread—and many cases are a result of nervous exhaustion, constant tension and the psychological conflicts often found in people who do intellectual work. Many eminent persons whom we honour for their outstanding achievements suffered mental illness during some period of their lives. Gogol spent his last years in a depressed state. Dostoevsky was an epileptic, and Chekhov had hallucinations due to overwork. The famous British biologist T. H. Huxley writes in his autobiography that he had been very handicapped by the need to seek periodic treatment for depressive psychosis. In the last twenty years of his life Charles Darwin suffered from mental illness never properly diagnosed but thought to be the result of tropical encephalitis with which he had been ill as a young man. Guy de Maupassant spent the last years of his life in a psychiatric clinic. Mayakovsky, Essenin, Fadeev, Hemingway, Jack London, Ordzhonikidze, Sabinin—a few examples among many other noted persons—all killed themselves in a state of mental depression. As for psychological abnormality, there are so many different kinds and many people suffer from one type or another during some period of their lives. Even chronic insomnia, which affected Lenin and considerably shortened his life, is an object of study for psychiatrists and can be treated in a mental hospital. According to the memoirs of Leo Tolstoy's relatives, he showed signs of mental illness in his sixties (see, for example, *Essay on the Past* by S. L. Tolstoy). Of course nobody can consider himself exempt from the possibility of falling prey to mental illness—there simply can be no guarantee against illness of any kind. And my purpose in writing the present work was certainly not to prove that there is *absolutely* nothing wrong with me. My aim is not so egocentric. It is rather to call attention to the dangerous tendency of using psychiatry for political purposes, the exploitation of medicine in an alien role as a means of intimidation and punishment—a new and illegal way of isolating people for their views and convictions. I also want to stress that psychiatrists must never be released from legal responsibility for their actions. In Nazi Germany, there was, as we all know, a state programme for the physical destruction of several categories of the mentally ill—and the psychiatric 'special examinations' carried out by Hitler's 'doctors' resulted in patients with severe or hereditary illness being sentenced to death in the gas chambers. At the Nuremberg Trials this practice was declared to be a *crime against humanity*.

What psychiatrists like Lunts, Bondareva, Lifshits, Leznenko and their protectors are beginning to do may be on different lines, but it is a move in the same general direction, and Soviet and world public opinion must be warned before it is too late.

Zhores Medvedev

August–September 1970
Obninsk

Postscript of 20 October 1970

On 12 October, the President of the Lenin Agricultural Academy, P. P. Lobanov, invited me to see him and told me that they had reconsidered the possibility of my working at their agricultural institute in Borovsk. On the next day the Institute formally accepted my appointment, and on 19 October I joined the staff as an acting senior research fellow in the laboratory of albumen and amino acids for a 'month's trial'. It remains to be seen what account a scientist can give of himself during a month's probation, but I hope I may pass the test.[1]

[1] At the time of going to press, he still holds this post.

10

Not Psycho-adaptation but Democratisation

ROY MEDVEDEV

THE present Minister of Health, B. Petrovsky, speaking before a group of young doctors at the very beginning of 1953, called on his listeners to repudiate outdated ideas about the role of the doctor in society and to master the ideals of 'Stalinist humanism'. The obstinacy shown by this erstwhile advocate of 'Stalinist humanism' in his support of the Kaluga psychiatrists, as well as the very extensive nature of the disciplinary meetings begun on 17 June, indicate that the illegal committal of my brother to a mental hospital was not just an isolated incident—rather it heralded a new phase in the dangerous escalation of the political abuse of psychiatry. This in turn is only part of the attempt by certain reactionary and conservative elements still influential in our leadership to halt the development of a very widespread mood among Soviet intellectuals and to thwart the long overdue democratisation of our social and political life.

One of the most serious inadequacies of our present political structure is that it is based on the assumption of total ideological uniformity throughout society. No provision is made for divergent views, and normal dialogue cannot take place within the Party or outside. This gives rise to such abnormalities as dismissals, trials and even psychiatric treatment as a means of political reprisal. We are concerned in the first instance with the problem of political dissent, although things are not easier for those who deviate from generally accepted standards in many other areas of intellectual and artistic life.

To avoid misrepresentation, let me state at once that when I refer to the political structure, I do not mean socialism in general or the Soviet social and political system, but rather that specific form of government which took shape in our country during the 1930s and 1940s and which in many ways negates the very principles of socialism and Soviet power. Of course the system has not remained static since that time. There were many changes after the Twentieth and Twenty-Second Party Congresses and after the October Plenum of the Central Committee.[1] But these changes did not go deep enough, and it is still possible for certain highly influential individuals not only to dream of a return to the old order, but to use the most disreputable methods in an attempt to revive the Stalin system in a somewhat modified form.

It must be stressed that the defects of our political structure are in no way distinctive features of the Soviet socialist state or inherent to it. These defects can and must be corrected within the framework of Soviet socialist society, and this will give our political and economic system not only more flexibility but also make it stronger and more stable.

Once and for all it must be understood that a regime

[1] See above, page 52.

which outlaws and persecutes political dissent as a matter of principle can be neither strong nor stable. This kind of intolerance is a sign not of strength, but of weakness, and it is particularly out of place today.

It is wrong to think that political differences cannot exist or are abnormal in a socialist society, especially at the present stage of human development, with so many vastly different ideological and political systems in the world and with the unprecedented speed and efficiency of mass means of communication. Never has it been so true that ideas know no boundaries. Under these circumstances it is entirely natural and normal for there to be differences of political opinion among Soviet citizens, especially since there are still differences in the material and social position of the various classes and groups within our society. There are also the enormous after-effects of Stalinism still apparent in the ideology, psychology and standards of behaviour of Soviet man, particularly many of the Party and state functionaries. Some have overcome this influence more quickly than others, while others cannot get rid of it even now.

Under present conditions there will certainly be differing views, apart from the official one, on a variety of political problems. In other words, political minorities are bound to exist, and they should have the right and possibility of expressing their views.

But the main point is that the problems which constantly crop up before the leadership of our country—political, foreign, economic, social, techno-logical—are of such enormous complexity, that there must be a study of alternatives, and different ideas must be tested out even in the political sphere. Yet such experimentation is unthinkable without freedom of debate and discussion, without the clash of different points of view. The right to express an opinion must be safeguarded not only until the majority makes its decision but also afterwards. It is completely intolerable to regard any difference in ideology or political opinion as 'ideological sabotage' or to call for repression and punishment rather than discussion and dialogue.

As we all know, only the socialist revolution put into practice the main principle of democracy: government on behalf of and in the interests of the majority of the people. However, while striving to achieve this most important democratic principle, we have not paid enough attention either in the past or in the present to another equally important one—the right of the minority to express and defend its own point of view. A society cannot be genuinely democratic if the right of the majority to govern is not secure, if the majority is unable to take decisions and implement them. However, neither can there be genuine democracy if the right to express and defend minority opinion is also not protected. This is important not only for the minority but also for the majority, for the whole of society. The majority might be wrong and the minority right. Views which today are shared only by a small number of people might be overwhelmingly accepted tomorrow, particularly since in a socialist country, the minority are in no sense exploiters. The fact is that individuals vary in their understanding of different aspects of socialism and communism, or of the concepts as a whole. Furthermore, within the framework of a single socialist programme, there can be a variety of views about tactics. Disagreements can arise about many questions which, though of minor importance in the long run, seem very important and highly controversial in the present. In all such cases it is necessary to protect not only the rights of the majority but those of the minority as well. The right of dissent should not be thought peculiar to bourgeois democracy. It is a most important feature of any democracy. There are exceptional situations in which certain important democratic freedoms, including freedom of speech and of opposition, can be temporarily restricted. Such a situation really did exist in our country during the first years of Soviet rule, but there was no reason for this state of emergency to apply during the building of socialism and communism. In today's world, fifty-three years after the October Revolution, it is certainly both absurd and extremely harmful to be intolerant towards dissent and opposition, political or otherwise.

In any society, once the need for it has arisen, a new political trend is bound to make itself felt despite all attempts to forbid or suppress it.

After the Twentieth and Twenty-Second Party Congresses and the October Plenum, Soviet society was confronted with so many complicated political problems, the Soviet people found themselves asking so many questions to which official propaganda gave no reply, that the emergence of a great variety of new political attitudes, subsequently translated into political trends, became quite inevitable. Such trends did in fact appear and they continue to grow, increasingly leaving their mark on the political life of the country, despite all efforts to ignore or conceal them. These different political attitudes can be found in the working class, among the peasantry and in the Party and state apparatus. However, they are most pronounced among the intellectuals who have better means of articulating their thoughts in political or literary form.

This is not the place to list and analyse all the political trends in question—they may be progressive or reactionary, 'right' or 'left', moderate or radical, constructive, anarchist, nationalist or chauvinist, 'Westernising' or 'slavophil',[1] rooted in Marxism or representing a new departure from it. I wish to observe, however, that although all these trends are now here to stay, our political structure lacks any normal mechanism for dialogue between majority and minority, between government and opposition, or even among the various different trends themselves. The consequences are both abnormal and ugly.

On the one hand, the advocates of various minority views, denied the possibility of expressing and defending their opinions, are often compelled to resort to all sorts of strategems—circulating their materials and documents in typescript or photocopies, publishing them abroad, etc. On the other hand, the guardians of the official point of view, frightened by the very existence of dissent and opposition, begin to seek different ways of suppressing and uprooting it. Feeling unable either to countenance the gradual development of socialist democracy and recognition of rights for political minorities, or, for very understandable

[1] These terms were originally applied in the 1840s when Russian intellectuals were divided into those who sought a solution to Russia's problems in the adoption of Western ideas and institutions, and those who favoured a 'national' solution.

reasons, to revive the Stalinist terror and to restore punitive functions to the security services by giving them the requisite powers, some of the highest Party and government officials have begun in recent years to devise roundabout ways of suppressing opposition, of terrorising and intimidating it. And, clearly, one such new method of conducting a 'dialogue' with dissenters, still in its experimental stage, is the 'psychiatric' approach. This was one of the things shown by Zhores's case. But an even more important lesson to be drawn from it is that the success or failure of such criminal experiments depends on the attitude and behaviour of all of us.

I should mention that there are several different ways in which mental hospitals are used to deal with 'awkward' citizens. I cannot dwell here on how psychiatrists treat people who are really ill, although in this respect also there seem to be grounds for uneasiness. There are many types of mental illness where compulsory treatment in a hospital or clinic is completely unnecessary. The patient is not a danger to himself or those around him, and usually only one particular area of his mind is affected, so that he is not prevented from more or less coping with his professional and family obligations. One such case was that of a certain B. who for five years regularly sent letters to Tvardovsky at *Novy Mir*, invariably beginning 'Dear Friedrich' and signed 'Karl Marx'. These letters usually discussed the problem of creating a world government with Marx and Engels at the head, flanked by a hundred deputies of different nationalities to assist them. This was so obviously a case of delusion that nobody thought it necessary to put B. in a psychiatric hospital. However, in a number of other instances it would seem that quite harmless cases like this have been hospitalised, against their own will and the wishes of their families, as dangerous to the public. I do not presume to judge whether or not this is right—and am only demanding here that there must be a careful examination of each such case by specialists. My main concern at the moment is the use of psychiatric hospitals to persecute persons who are to all intents and purposes healthy.

There are cases of people being committed to a mental hospital who many years before had indeed suffered some slight psychological disorder, but were cured and are now perfectly well. If for some reason or another a person like this falls foul of his local authorities, they are quite capable of bringing up his long forgotten illness as grounds for forcible committal. This recently happened to a good friend of mine in Leningrad, Igor N. Twenty-five years before, when he was a student at Leningrad State University, Igor fell ill due to overwork and was placed by his family in a mental hospital. In ten months he was well again and returned to his studies. He graduated from university brilliantly, defended a Master's dissertation and completed the preparations for a doctorate. Being an independent and honest person, N. was always willing to discuss even the most 'delicate' problems with his students, for example, the expulsion of the historian Nekrich[1] from the Party, the fate of

---

[1] A. Nekrich was expelled from the Party because of his book about the origins of World War II, *June 1941*, which gave a frank account of Stalin's failure to prepare the country for war. The book was the subject of an acrimonious debate in 1966 at the Institute of History of the Academy of Sciences, and was later published in France.

F. F. Raskolnikov[1] and his 'Open Letter', and the question of Stalin and his crimes. All this very much displeased the authorities at the institute where he taught, and when they learned that he was writing some sort of letter addressed to the coming Twenty-Fourth Party Congress, it was the last straw. With the approval of Tolstikov,[2] N. was arrested and then subjected to compulsory psychiatric examination. They refurbished the diagnosis of twenty-five years before and used it to have him sent for compulsory 'treatment' to a prison psychiatric hospital. A mere three months later, Igor N. was released from the hospital as 'cured', however he was kept under permanent psychiatric supervision as an outpatient. Significantly, although N.'s behaviour was officially declared the result of 'illness', he was expelled from the Party after his release from the hospital and barred from a teaching career.

Mental hospitals have also been used in recent years as a way of dealing with certain people who had previously been arrested, and charged under Articles 70 ('anti-Soviet agitation and propaganda') or 190 (1) and 190 (3) ('dissemination of deliberately slanderous fabrication defaming the Soviet state and society or gross breach of public order') of the Criminal Code.

Some prominent Soviet intellectuals believe that the provisions of these articles of the Criminal Code conflict with the Constitution which guarantees freedom of speech and the freedom to demonstrate to all

[1] F. F. Raskolnikov, Soviet Ambassador to Bulgaria, defected to France in 1937 and committed suicide in 1939.

[2] V. Tolstikov was Party boss of Leningrad. He had a reputation for dealing harshly with dissident intellectuals. In 1970 he was made ambassador to Peking.

citizens of our country. But given that Articles 70 and 190 have the force of law, there are great difficulties in applying them as legal sanctions for the prosecution of dissenters. First of all, the prosecution must show that the defendant's opinions are false, or constitute anti-Soviet propaganda, rather than criticism of real shortcomings, whether past or present. This is no easy task, especially if the accused reminds his judges about those terrible crimes which were committed under Stalin not only by individual political leaders but also by many government organisations. The accused may also bring up many of the misguided measures taken in Khrushchev's time—in economics, in politics, in diplomacy and in military policy, in the field of culture and education, in Party and state administration, etc. Secondly, the prosecution must show that the views or materials complained of were *deliberate* fabrications—that is, that the accused acted with malice aforethought and disseminated the information or views in question with the deliberate aim of undermining or weakening the Soviet system. Legal commentary on the application of Article 70 particularly stresses that 'the prosecution of people called for criticism, dissatisfaction, or disagreement with some measure or another of the Party and government authorities is impermissible, and contradicts the substance of the law'. 'An individual is accountable for anti-Soviet agitation and propaganda only *in those cases* when he *deliberately* disseminates views about the Soviet state or society that he knows to be false, and that they defame or discredit . . .' Furthermore 'in order to find a person guilty of anti-Soviet agitation and propaganda, it must be established that the slanderous fabrication, discrediting the Soviet social and political order, has been disseminated by him with the intention of undermining the Soviet system. There is no case for a charge of anti-Soviet agitation and propaganda if a person is honestly mistaken in the interpretation of some aspect or other of Soviet life or in his view of the political institutions of the Soviet state, etc. This kind of error, for example, can be the result of incorrect information.' There is a similar commentary on Article 190 (see M. P. Mikhailov and V. V. Nazarov: *Ideological Sabotage—A Weapon of Imperialism*, Law Publishing House, Moscow 1969, pp. 44–5, 47, 57). In other words, there has to be a proof of intent as well as of the objective facts of the case. And this is a very difficult task for the prosecution —at least it has not managed to cope with it in any of the political trials during the last five years. At all these trials the speeches for the defence were incomparably more convincing than the speeches for the prosecution. And as we know, though they ended with the accused being sentenced, in most of the cases the absence of legal grounds was obvious and the moral victory was invariably on the side of the accused. No wonder that the public reaction both in the Soviet Union and abroad was extremely negative, so that in the end these trials had very different results from those envisaged by their organisers. It was awareness of this that gave rise in certain quarters to the idea that rather than bring such cases to trial in open court, it would be better first to draw up an indictment and then demand a psychiatric examination. The accused person would then be declared unfit to stand trial and instead of going to prison would be put in a special mental hospital for compulsory 'treatment'. The court session can thus take place without the presence of the accused or the public, and the whole task of intimidating and punishing dissenters would seem to be much simpler. This is just the way in which former Major-General Petr Grigorenko was sentenced to 'treatment' for an indefinite period, and at the moment he is being held in a psychiatric prison-hospital recently built in Chernyakhovsk.[1]

It is obvious to me that both the court's decision and the findings of the 'special examination' were ill-founded in the case of Grigorenko. In 1968 and 1969 I met Grigorenko several times. We had a particularly long and involved conversation at the end of April 1969, that is, only a few days before his arrest. He is clearly an extraordinary and absolutely normal man in complete command of his faculties. Much of what he said seemed to me mistaken, and I told him so. I couldn't accept his favourable view of Avtorkhanov's[2] book which is full of all kinds of invention and misrepresentation. Some of Grigorenko's proposals, especially in his open letters to the Procurator-General, the Chairman of the KGB, the international conference of Communist leaders in Budapest,[3] and others, seemed to me unrealistic. I told Grigorenko that some

[1] (Author's footnote.) In addition to the two psychiatric prison-hospitals in Leningrad and Kazan, which significantly are not under the jurisdiction of the Ministry of Health, several similar institutions have been created in the last few years. I have been told that many wards in these institutions are for the time being empty—they still await their patients. Meanwhile many people who are really ill cannot receive the treatment they need because normal psychiatric clinics are overburdened.

[2] A. Avtorkhanov, Soviet citizen, now living in exile. Author of a study of the Soviet regime entitled *The Technology of Power*.

[3] Held shortly before the invasion of Czechoslovakia.

of his views reminded me of the Anarcho-Communists of 1918–20. He argued with me, but without a trace of intolerance and agreed with some of my objections. He made no attempt to impose his own views on me and recognised that there could be other approaches to the problems which concerned him. With certain reservations, Grigorenko's views can be described as extremely radical. But clearly it is a question of a *system of views* and not of mental health. Any argument with Grigorenko can be conducted only by means of political dialogue, not with the aid of compulsory hospitalisation.[1]

[1] (Author's footnote.) At the opposite end of our political spectrum we encounter another kind of extremism, which is more dangerous in every way than the extremism of Grigorenko and some of those who share his views. I have in mind people like Kochetov [a neo-Stalinist whose novels *The Brothers Yershov* (1958) and *What do you Wish* (1969) are crude lampoons on the liberal intelligentsia] and Shevtsov [see above, page 44]. Their political programme is clearly expressed in their novels and is shared, unfortunately, by a significant number of Party and State officials. It is an unreal and reactionary utopia, infinitely removed from the actual needs and demands of our society. Some readers of their most recent novels find clear signs of mental illness in them. There are so many crude distortions of Soviet reality that if the element of mental illness is excluded, then it can only be a matter of 'deliberately slandering the Soviet state and society'. In Kochetov's novels there are clear signs of both persecution mania and megalomania, and in those of Shevtsov it is easy to find pathological anti-semitism as well. However, we do not agree with the view which some people hold that on these grounds Kochetov and Shevtsov have to be considered mentally ill. People like Kochetov and Shevtsov are unable to understand the new situation in our country; they cannot adjust to new demands or 'adapt' to the changed social environment. Realising the discrepancy between their own views and real life, witnessing the collapse of their former extravagant pretensions, these people find themselves in a state near to panic. This explains their pathological fear in the face of reality, their hysteria, their efforts to distort the facts and in this way to mislead the Soviet leadership, inciting them to extreme measures. However, despite the inability of Shevtsov and Kochetov to 'adapt', we are not dealing with mental illness but with a system of views, this time not radical but extremely reactionary ones. And the struggle against them can only be pursued by political and ideological means without the help of psychiatric hospitals.

Similar treatment was meted out to Ivan Yakh-imovich, one of the best collective farm chairmen in Latvia, and known to be an honest and principled Communist. At the beginning of 1968 Yakhimovich sent a letter to Suslov protesting against the political trial of Ginsburg[1] and others. It was a sharp but entirely sincere document, full of concern for the prestige of our Party and for the fate of socialist democracy. Yakhimovich's letter attracted a great deal of attention but it simply resulted in the unjust persecution of him as well—he was removed from his position as collective farm chairman and later expelled from the Party. He was forced to work as a loader to keep his family. In August 1968 Yakhimovich wrote a letter vigorously protesting against the invasion of Czechoslovakia by the Warsaw Pact troops. Soon after this he was arrested. But his interrogators were unable to prepare a plausible indictment against Yakhimovich. It was quite obvious that he had criticised not the Party and government as such, but only particular measures and decisions. Yet in the legal commentary on the application of Article 190 (1) it says specifically that 'this article cannot be applied to expressions of dissatisfaction or disagreement with individual measures or actions of the Party, the government, or their agencies. Dissatisfaction or disagreement themselves cannot be regarded as criminal since such attitudes come within the sphere of a person's inner convictions and characterise his view of particular social and political measures only . . .' (Mikhailov and Nazarov,

---

[1] The principal charge against Alexander Ginsburg and his friends was that they had organised protests against the Sinyavsky–Daniel trial of 1965 and compiled a 'White Book' of documents about it.

p. 56). It was also obvious that the prosecution would not be able to prove intent as required by Article 190. Yakhimovich had not disseminated any kind of deliberate slander—he had only expressed his own view, absolutely convinced of its correctness.

It was therefore decided to pursue the Yakhimovich case along psychiatric lines. The first psychiatric examination took place in Riga, but although they found 'paranoid disorder', the grounds given for the diagnosis were so absurd that the Riga court called for a second examination. The psychiatrists, in listing the 'peculiarities' of Yakhimovich's behaviour, said that he 'puts the public interest higher than his own', 'believes that he has to dedicate his own life to the ideals of communism', 'wears a beard', 'thinks that the entry of the Warsaw Pact troops into Czechoslovakia was aggression', etc. The second examination took place in Moscow at the Serbsky Institute, after he had spent a hundred days in a Moscow prison. The Serbsky Institute confirmed the diagnosis of the Latvian psychiatrists, but dressed it up in psychiatric terminology. After this a second court sentenced him *in absentia* to compulsory 'treatment until recovery'. In order to avoid being given injections, he had to agree to take tablets, apparently the same powerful depressants that had been offered to my brother by Lifshits. In an attempt to break Yakhimovich's will, the 'doctors' put him in a ward with violent and dangerously aggressive patients who tried to attack him. Recently he was transferred to a quieter ward and allowed to receive visits from his family.[1]

How many more such cases are there of healthy

[1] He was released in the spring of 1971. See above, page 16.

people being put into mental hospitals? This could only be established by a thorough public investigation.

My brother's case clearly marked a new phase in the abuse of psychiatry for political purposes. There was no criminal charge against him, he was neither brought to court nor put under arrest. The only pretext for his committal was some anonymous criticism of his writings on the problems of science. But these works are not political, and are no more than studies of certain obstacles to the normal development of Soviet science. They were based on a painstaking investigation of the facts, and it would have been difficult to prove unintended error, let alone deliberate falsehood. There were simply no grounds for an arrest or prosecution. Therefore some authority— we still do not know which, but clearly it was not a legal one—decided to resort to psychiatric violence. This action created a potential threat for the whole of our intelligentsia, which is why it aroused such enormous indignation and particularly sharp and widespread protests.

Yet the success of this short though very intensive campaign in defence of Zhores is still far from complete. One can imagine that even without it, within a few months Zhores would have been released from the hospital after being declared 'abnormal' and subjected to compulsory 'treatment'. Thanks to the mass protests, Zhores was released after only nineteen days and without any kind of 'treatment'. But he was nevertheless declared 'abnormal' and registered in a psychiatric outpatient department. This means that his work as a publicist and sociologist can henceforth be represented as the product of schizoid or paranoid delusion—if not to the public at large, then at least in the more restricted circles of Party and government officials, and during propaganda briefings. The organisers of this disgraceful action had not reckoned with such a stormy reaction from scientists both in the Soviet Union and abroad. That is why they cut short Zhores's stay in hospital and did not resort to compulsory 'treatment'. However they did not abandon their main purpose—to brand Zhores as abnormal, and by keeping him under the constant threat of a repeat performance, to reduce him to silence and put an end to his publicist activities. In these circumstances we would only be aiding and abetting the whole criminal operation if we were not to speak up. It is still uncertain how we can try to have the Kaluga hospital's 'diagnosis' revoked—it was evidently approved by the Ministry of Health. In our country medicine is a hierarchical service, where the opinion of the higher authority is almost always binding on the lower. But at any event we are certain that a full account of all that happened to my brother in May and June 1970 is the best proof of how totally absurd the 'diagnosis' was. It will also help our public to understand similar cases.

The danger is not over, and many people are still in psychiatric hospitals for political reasons. An even larger number live under the threat of psychiatric reprisal. Who will be next? It is no idle question.

In 1920 Zamyatin wrote a futuristic novel, *We*, describing a society in which every dissident was automatically declared abnormal.

The American science fiction writer Robert Sheckley wrote a story called 'The Academy' several years ago, in which he described an imaginary country where the government considers its main task to be the preservation of the *status quo* and to this end keeps a constant check on the mental health of all its citizens. In all offices and private apartments, in restaurants and public institutions of this country, there are gauges for the measurement of sanity. These instruments have a scale numbered from 0 to 10 which makes it possible to establish the degree of an individual's potential danger to the social order. 0 is the theoretically ideal psychic state in which the individual is a completely obedient cog in the state machine, harbouring not the slightest wish to change the existing order. Anything above 0 indicates deviation from the norm. But the range from 0 to 3 is considered permissible and does not require the interference of a doctor. If the gauge shows 4 to 7, then the person must go immediately to a therapist for consultation. A citizen whose reading is higher than 7 is considered to be potentially dangerous to those around him and is obliged by law to be registered and then, in the course of a trial period, to lower his number at least to 7. If he does not succeed, then he must undergo surgical change of the personality. If the pointer of the gauge crosses the red line at the number 10, then there cannot be any question of normal therapy and surgery becomes compulsory; or the luckless citizen must go for 'treatment' to the special 'medical' department of the Academy, which guarantees a hundred per cent cure, but from which, for some reason, nobody ever returns. Further on we learn that in the Academy the restless individual who hankers for change is given a special injection after which he falls asleep for ever. But before death, in a dream, in the world of illusion, he realises the fulfilment of all the wishes and plans which had given him no peace before he entered the Academy.

The social systems described by Zamyatin and Sheckley may sound like sheer fantasy, but the increasing frequency in recent years of psychiatric reprisals suggest that there are some people in our country who would like nothing more than to govern with the aid of psychiatry and measuring instruments. And we must frustrate these ambitions from the very beginning. They really are, after all, a public danger.

A NOTE ON THE TYPE

The text of this book has been set on the Monotype in a type face named Bembo. The roman is a copy of a letter cut for the celebrated Venetian printer Aldus Manutius by Francesco Griffo, and first used in Cardinal Bembo's *De Aetna* of 1495 —hence the name of the revival. Griffo's type is now generally recognized, thanks to the researches of Mr. Stanley Morison, to be the first of the old face group of types. The companion italic is an adaptation of the chancery script type designed by the Roman calligrapher and printer Lodovico degli Arrighi, called Vincentino, and used by him during the 1520's.

This book was printed and bound by
The Haddon Craftsmen, Inc., Scranton, Pennsylvania.
Binding design by Christine Aulicino.